THE RIGHT WING INDIVIDUALIST
TRADITION IN AMERICA

The Right Wing Individualist Tradition in America

Advisory Editors:

Dr. Murray N. Rothbard,
Polytechnic Institute of Brooklyn
Jerome Tuccille,
New School for Social Research

POISON DROPS IN THE FEDERAL SENATE.

THE

SCHOOL QUESTION

FROM A

PARENTAL AND NON-SECTARIAN STAND-POINT.

AN EPITOME OF THE EDUCATIONAL VIEWS

OF

ZACH. MONTGOMERY,

ON ACCOUNT OF WHICH VIEWS A STUBBORN BUT FRUITLESS EFFORT WAS MADE
IN THE UNITED STATES SENATE TO PREVENT HIS CONFIRMATION
AS ASSISTANT ATTORNEY-GENERAL.

WITHDRAWN

*Compiled by himself from the United States Census Reports
and from his own writings.*

Arno Press & The New York Times
New York · 1972

Reprint Edition 1972 by Arno Press Inc.

LC# 72-172221
ISBN 0-405-00430-3

The Right Wing Individualist Tradition in America
ISBN for complete set: 0-405-00410-9
See last pages of this volume for titles.

Manufactured in the United States of America

POISON DROPS IN THE FEDERAL SENATE.

THE

SCHOOL QUESTION

FROM A

PARENTAL AND NON-SECTARIAN STAND-POINT.

AN EPITOME OF THE EDUCATIONAL VIEWS

OF

ZACH. MONTGOMERY,

ON ACCOUNT OF WHICH VIEWS A STUBBORN BUT FRUITLESS EFFORT WAS MADE
IN THE UNITED STATES SENATE TO PREVENT HIS CONFIRMATION
AS ASSISTANT ATTORNEY-GENERAL.

*Compiled by himself from the United States Census Reports
and from his own writings.*

FOURTH EDITION.

WASHINGTON:
GIBSON BROS., PRINTERS AND BOOKBINDERS.
1889

Massachusetts crime column in 1860, 1 criminal to every 649 people.

Virginia's crime column in 1860, 1 criminal to every 6,566.

In order to prevent crime Massachusetts, as early as 1647, gave the educational control of children to the public, and after over 200 years trial, to wit, in 1860, she had 1 native white criminal to every 649 people.

Virginia, down to 1860, had always left the educational control of children to their fathers and mothers, and the result was 1 criminal to every 6,566 inhabitants.

For proof of similar results wherever the parental and anti-parental systems have been tried read this book. Herein will be found the record evidence which the late Richard Grant White, of N. Y., declared—

" Proves the case against the public-school system as clearly and undeniably as the truth of Newton's theory of gravitation is proved by the calculations which enable astronomers to declare the motions and weigh the substance of the planets."

(See North American Review, Dec., 1880.)

CONTENTS.

CHAPTER I.

INTRODUCTORY—THE SCHOOL QUESTION IN THE UNITED STATES SENATE—
DEMAND FOR THIS PUBLICATION—CORRESPONDENCE WITH SENATORS
INGALLS AND EDMUNDS—STRONG AND ABLE ENDORSEMENTS BY WASH-
INGTON PROTESTANT MINISTERS AND OTHERS.

THE vigorous and bitter fight made in the United States Senate against the author during the 49th session of Congress for the purpose of preventing his confirmation as Assistant Attorney-General, because of his views on the school question, seems to have awakened a very general desire in the public mind to know just what those views are.

So frequent and so urgent have been the demands upon him—by letters and otherwise—for information on this subject, that he finally determined to meet this demand by republishing " DROPS FROM THE POISON FOUNTAIN," enlarged by the addition of certain other articles of his recently published in " THE FAMILY'S DEFENDER."

This course seems the more necessary in view of the fact that some of those who supported his appointment have been called upon, and others are liable to be called upon, to justify their action in maintaining in official position a man entertaining such sentiments upon this educational question and kindred subjects as have been charged—and some of them *falsely charged* upon the writer.

Senator Ingalls, of Kansas, charged the writer with having given utterance to sentiments such as were not only unpatriotic, but utterly incompatible both with his duties as a citizen and his oath as an officer of the Government.

But it will also be remembered that Mr. Ingalls did *not* tell the Senate nor the public that his only authority for making these charges was an anonymous pamphlet published in the city of San Francisco in 1873 in order to advance the partisan ends of a most intolerant band of anti-Catholic proscriptionists. Neither did the Senator reveal the fact that said publication was, at the time of its appearance, branded as false in a published card signed by more than a dozen as respectable gentlemen as could be found in said city.

In a letter addressed by that writer to Mr. Ingalls relative to said charge, he said :

" I am free to admit that if I had ever uttered or entertained the infamous sentiments you and your anonymous author attribute to me,

I would not only be unfit to hold office, but unworthy the countenance of all honorable and intelligent people. If the 'No-Popery' cry is to be the weapon with which my enemies propose to fight me, I trust that in future it may be an honest cry of, at least, seeming truth, backed by as much as *one* reputable name, and not resting *solely* on the false charges of an anonymous scribbler."

During this contest, in order to meet boldly and fairly the opposition which was being made to the writer, either because of the views falsely attributed to him, or because of his real views as expressed in "DROPS FROM POISON FOUNTAIN," he sent a copy of said last-named pamphlet to every member of the Senate.

Accompanying each pamphlet was a letter of which the following, to Mr. Senator Edmunds, chairman of the Senate Judiciary Committee, is a fair sample, to wit:

DEPARTMENT OF THE INTERIOR,
ASSISTANT ATTORNEY-GENERAL'S OFFICE.
WASHINGTON, D. C., *March 1st*, 1886.

Hon. GEO. F. EDMUNDS.

DEAR SIR: Enclosed please find a pamphlet of my production, which, as I gather from Saturday's *Washington Star*, expresses sentiments such as a majority of the Senate Judiciary Committee suppose to be sufficient proof of my unfitness for the office of Assistant Attorney-General.

I cannot help thinking that the action of the committee must have been based on a mistaken notion as to the contents of this pamphlet, for whoever will carefully read it must see that its very *life* and *soul* and *power*, for good or evil, lie in its truly startling statistics of crime. *These* have with great care and at some expense been compiled from the United States Census Reports. In proof of the correctness of my figures, I beg leave to refer you to the testimony of the late distinguished Richard Grant White, of New York, which you will find in a marginal note on page 5 of the accompanying pamphlet. If for publishing these statistics at my own expense I deserve to be forever ostracised from office, then what can be said in defence of those Hon. Senators and Representatives who originally enacted the law requiring these very same statistics to be gathered and printed at the *people's* expense?

I have no apology to make for the publication of this pamphlet. Indeed, so important do I regard the work of making known its facts and figures to the American people, that nothing but my poverty prevents me from placing it gratuitously in the hands of every man, woman, and school-child in the United States, for I am fully persuaded that a general knowledge of these facts and figures would result in such a reformation in our public educational system as to place it in harmony with the God-ordained relations between parents and children. And this is *all* the reformation I ever desired or advocated. Be kind enough to examine this pamphlet and notify

me of anything you may find therein tending to prove my unfitness
for the office of Assistant Attorney.General, and much oblige,

Yours, most respectfully,

Zach. Montgomery.

No answer to the above letter was ever received.

The pamphlet referred to in the last preceding letter will be found
incorporated into this little volume. It was concerning the matter
contained in that same pamphlet that the Hon. Peter H. Burnett,
California's first Governor under American rule, and one of the
most eminent of her Supreme Court Judges, in a letter addressed to
the author, said:

" *It is one of the most conclusive arguments I have ever read
upon any disputed subject.*"

The late Mr. Richard Grant White, of N. Y., who professed
neither the religious nor political faith of the author, but who was
a gentleman distinguished throughout the whole country for his
learning, ability, and great accuracy as a writer, published in the
North American Review for Dec., 1880, a carefully prepared article entitled

" The Public-School Failure."

The leading facts upon which Mr. White based his article—as he
tells us himself—were taken from said pamphlet. In a foot-note to
said article he says:

" My attention was directed to these facts by a pamphlet on the
system of anti-parental education, by the Hon. Zachary Montgomery, of California, which I received on the 23d of October last, after
the publication of my articles on the public schools in the *New
York Times*. Mr. Montgomery's trenchant pamphlet contains very
elaborate tables, made up from the United States Census Reports. *I
have verified them by those reports, and find them essentially accurate and trustworthy.*"

As introductory to Mr. White's quotations from our tabulated
statistics, he characterizes them as

" *Evidence which proves the case against the public-school system as clearly and as undeniably as the truth of Newton's theory
of gravitation is proved by the calculations which enable astronomers to declare the motions and weigh the substance of the planets.*"

And yet, for the publication of *that evidence*, and the drawing
therefrom deductions which are as irresistible as that two and two
make four, the author has been denounced upon the floor of an
American Senate, and throughout the country by a certain class

of politicians, as if he were unfit to live in any civilized community, and much less fit to be entrusted with any public office whatever. And all this, too—be it remembered—was done in the name of *education*, civilization, liberty, and progress ! ! !

Let the reader peruse the following pages, and then decide whether it is the author or his accusers that deserve the anathemas that have been heaped upon the head of the former.

VIEWS OF PROMINENT PROTESTANT CLERGYMEN OF WASHINGTON, AND ELSE-
WHERE, CALLED FORTH BY READING THE FIRST EDITION OF THIS WORK.

Soon after its first publication copies of this work were sent to a considerable number of Protestant clergymen, and an expression of opinion relative to its position on the school question was asked for.

The following letters and extracts from letters received in reply clearly demonstrate the non-sectarian character of the principles herein maintained, and show that they are sufficiently broad and liberal in their nature to challenge the approval of intelligent and honest people of every creed under the sun.

METHODIST EPISCOPAL VIEWS.

Rev. Dr. John H. Dashiell, a prominent Methodist minister of Washington, after reading this book, wrote, saying :

" Schools can never take the place of home. Americans must not become Spartans. Freedom, representative government, and home abide together. Whatever tends to destroy parental influence is fatal to society and church and government."

Rev. John P. Newman, since made a Methodist bishop, and one of the most widely-known preachers of his church in the United States, January 15, 1887, wrote :

" Thanks for your able pamphlet, which I read last night. All I ought to say now on the subject is this : I agree with your fundamental position in the abstract, that education of the child is the duty and right of the parent ; but the concrete is not possible now ; therefore the State should do what parents cannot or will not do."

EPISCOPALIAN VIEWS.

Rev. John B. Williams, a talented and influential Episcopalian minister of Bladensburg, near Washington, Jan. 12, 1887, after reading the book, wrote :

" Years ago I lost all confidence in our secularized system, apart from the great constitutional objections with which you so justly assail it. God's way can never be abandoned without alarming results following. The principles enunciated have been mine for years; the facts are new and startling."

Rev. Dr. W. A. Leonard, one of Washington's most distinguished Episcopalian clergymen, Jan. 13, 1887, wrote, saying:

" To your basal principle of parental right no one surely can hesitate to give assent, as you have presented and qualified or guarded it. If the criminal statistics grow, logically, out of the godlessness of our public education, there can be no question as to the vital importance of probing the wound down to the quick. My own position is a simple one. Education without christian religion as its leaven is as dangerous as a sharp-edged tool in the hands of a child."

Very similar sentiments were expressed by Rev. John W. Philips, Rev. John S. Lindsay, and Rev. J. S. Townsend.

A BAPTIST VIEW OF THE BOOK.

March 29, 1887, Rev. G. W. McCullough, a distinguished Baptist minister of Washington, wrote, saying:

" I have given some time and study to the school question as set forth by you, and I believe I can say I can endorse your platform of education with this exception—the taking out of our schools the Bible. I cannot see the wisdom or advantage of this."

Another careful reading of the book would doubtless have satisfied the reverend gentleman that our platform neither proposes to take the Bible out nor to take it into the schools, but to protect the parent in his sacred right to select for his *own* children a school either with the Bible or without the Bible, just as he pleases.

A LUTHERAN VIEW.

Rev. S. Domer, a well-known and highly-respected Lutheran minister of Washington, Jan. 19, 1887, wrote, saying, *inter alia :*

" Superficial as my examination has necessarily been, I have risen from the reading very favorably impressed.

" 1st. The platform : I like it. It seems to be radically principled in righteousness, and comprehensive enough to take in the entire range of the system. * * * The home, I most heartily agree, must be central in any advanced civilization and in any true system of education. The State should protect and cherish our familyhood in the highest degree, and in doing so give the largest freedom for the play of parental choices as to the educational and religious culture of children. No more reason why the State should control in education than religion. I thoroughly agree with you that parents should have the right to choose their own schools for their children as well as the churches to which they shall go. And duty must be in the same direction. I would be glad to see a grand reformation, or rather regeneration, in our school system of the character indicated in your book and platform."

A PRESBYTERIAN VIEW.

Rev. Dr. A. W. Pitzer, a Presbyterian minister of Washington of marked ability, Jan. 18, 1887, wrote, saying:

"Hearty thanks for your pamphlet. The present system of public schools is unconstitutional, unscriptural, and unnatural, and threatens our destruction in the future.

"On page 74 I endorse all you say, beginning with the words, 'I maintain,' etc., etc., and ending with the word 'educated,' six lines from the bottom. I would be glad to see you and compare views, and see if anything can be done to check the growing evil."

A copy of the book was sent to Rev. Dr. R. L. Dabney, one of the most eminent and widely-known Presbyterian ministers in America, and a Professor in the State University of Texas, and after reading it, he wrote as follows:

AUSTIN, TEXAS, *June* 21, 1887.

Hon. Z. MONTGOMERY.

DEAR SIR: I have to thank you very heartily for the present of your book upon the methods of primary State education. You can have no stronger assurance of the sincerity of these thanks than is contained in the fact that your able discussions substantiate every point I made 15 years ago in Virginia, when opposing the fastening of this vicious system on that State. Of course you experience the same species of unfair retorts which fell to my lot, which was to be constantly represented as an enemy of education, and of the elevation of the children of the masses. Every sensible man of course desires the true education and moral and mental advancement of all the young, and especially of the children of the poor. It has been my life's business to labor for this The question between us and the new-fangled men is only the question as to the safest and best methods for attaining this end, confessed by all to be a good one. Now, to confound this plainest of distinctions and charge a man with being hostile to the valued end only because he opposes vicious methods tending to disappoint the end itself, is a resort too coarse and vulgar to be very honest. Especially is it hard for an honest man to recognize any candor in this method of attack after you have so clearly demonstrated by facts that the new-fangled method does not attain the proposed end, but increases crime and ignorance.

A multitude of intelligent people throughout the country agree with you, of whom the most are afraid to show their heads. But telling exposures like yours will in time do their work. The real opposition which you have to meet is from the pecuniary self-interest of the vast office-holding class of school officials. They have effectually found out this fact, that whether the new-fangled system really educates the youth of the country or not it opens a nice, broad path for their hands into the pockets of the tax-payers, and gives them a nice, plausible pretext in the popular cry for the " glorious cause of education " to widen that path and keep it open. Hence this imperious jealousy of all discussion, this tyrannical denial of the right of free thought, upon this one topic. It has come to this—that although the journals may be freely opened to the most outrageous attacks of an Ingersoll upon everything sacred in christianity, no parent nor tax-payer is to be allowed to discuss the question whether this new-fangled method for educating his own children is safe and wise or not. Truly the Americans are a free people.

Very respectfully,

R. L. DABNEY.

A HEBREW VIEW.

Rev. L. Stern, a prominent Hebrew divine, and a hitherto admirer of the public-school system, March 1, 1887, wrote, saying:

" At the present moment it is quite impossible for me to give your work the careful perusal it certainly deserves, and which alone could possibly cause me to modify my notions in regard to our public-school system, which, its various faults notwithstanding, in the main I have always admired. My impression is that your ideas expressed in paragraph 4, p. 83, could form the basis for a satisfactory reconstruction of the present system."

A LETTER FROM A PUBLIC SCHOOL PRINCIPAL.

On the 12th of September, 1888, Professor J. B. Specking, principal of the public schools of Washington, Mo., addressed a letter to the author, in which, among other things, he said:

" I have just finished reading your little book on the school question for the second time. The more I have studied the matter the more convinced I have become that your position is the correct one. * * * But what troubles me most is this: Suppose that the whole business of teaching were thrown open to private enterprise, then since there are so many sects and factions each one of these would have to establish a school of its own; or, what seems to be the same, so many teachers would have to establish so many independent schools that it would be impossible to have anything like a graded system in towns of less than 10,000 inhabitants, while in country districts where they can scarcely afford to hire one teacher now, they, of course, could have no school at all. How could this difficulty be overcome? "

The following is a part of the author's reply:

" It seems to me that your question can be best answered by supposing a case. Let us then take a neighborhood consisting of ten families averaging four children each of school age. And in order to make your difficulty as formidable as possible, we will suppose that each of these ten families represents a denomination of religionists different from the others. Now you can truly say that in the case supposed it would be impossible for each of these families (upon the plan I propose) to have a teacher of its own denomination.

But it must be remembered that the plan for which I am contending does not rest on *denominational*, but on *parental* grounds; and even so far as the denominational question is concerned, not one of these ten families would be any worse off under the plan proposed than under the present public-school system, for, as you know, the public-school laws forbid, and necessarily forbid, the teaching of denominational doctrines in these schools. But while none of these ten families would, in a denominational point of view, fare any worse under the proposed plan than they now do under the existing system, it is easy to see that in a parental point of view they would fare much better, because the heads of these families could each exercise his own careful, conscientious judgment in the selection of the teacher who was to be entrusted with the sacred duty of moulding the character and to a large extent shaping the future destinies of his children. Neither would such a community be left long without a school. In proof of this, let us suppose that you yourself were seeking to establish a school in just such a community as that referred to; do you think that with your knowledge of human nature, and with your twelve years' experience in teaching, you would find it hard to secure the school patronage of every one of these families, even though you might differ religiously from them all? Of course, in undertaking to establish a school in such a community, it would be not only your duty, but your interest, to have it understood in advance that you would scrupulously avoid both the use of any books and the teaching of any principles antagonistic to the religious views of any class of people patronizing your school. If we suppose that you are known to such a community to be a man of deservedly good moral character, and a perfectly competent teacher of the secular branches, what parent could reasonably object to allowing you to teach his children these branches, in view of the impossibility of having them taught in a school of his own denomination? Most certainly the religious parent who could not safely educate his children in a non-sectarian school of his own selection could not safely nor consistently allow them to be educated in a non-sectarian school selected by a board of politicians. In other words, he could neither safely nor consistently allow them to be educated in a non-sectarian public school."

The above is only a brief extract from the author's answer to Professor Specking.

Some time afterwards, to wit, Nov. 28, 1888, the professor, in acknowledging its receipt, among other things, said:

"Your lengthy and full reply to the difficulties which I proposed satisfied me that your plan was superior to the present public-school system *in every respect*. So well satisfied am I of this that I have determined to leave the public-school service at an early date, and to organize a private school of my own. I shall also, in the future, spare no effort to educate the people to see this all-important subject in its true light. But random effort will do but little good; we must be united in this great cause of educational reform."

CHAPTER II.

CRIME IN PARENTAL AND ANTI-PARENTAL SCHOOL STATES COMPARED.

THE writer intends to offer no apology to the reading community for this publication. As soon would he think of apologizing to the slumbering inhabitants of a city in flames for attempting to disturb their rest by the vigorous ringing of a fire-bell. Far better that they awake even in anger, than to awake not at all.

If the reader will but follow us, even to the extent of a few pages, we promise to demonstrate, by incontestable facts and figures drawn from sources that will not and cannot be impeached, that the calamity at which we are endeavoring to alarm our countrymen is far more widespread and direful in its consequences than any conflagration that ever devastated a city. We promise to prove that our boasted New England public-school system, as now by law established throughout the length and breadth of the American Republic, is a poisonous fountain, fraught with the seeds of human misery and moral death. But, says the reader, how can that possibly be true? Can it be denied that an educated people are more-moral and virtu-ous, more contented, happy, and law-abiding than an ignorant peo-ple, and if so, how can it be charged that a system of education which almost entirely banishes illiteracy from the land is fraught with so much evil to those who are brought under its influence? These are candid questions, and they shall receive candid answers. It is very true that *ignorance is the mother of vice.* It is also true that an educated people, *if properly* educated, *are more* moral, virtuous, contented, happy, and law-abiding than an ignorant peo-ple.

Thus far, we think there can be no difference of opinion between the most inveterate supporter of the New England public-school system and ourselves.

Now, keeping steadily in view this common stand-point, namely, that a people *properly* educated *are* more moral, virtuous, contented, happy, and law-abiding than an ignorant people, let us suppose that we somewhere find living, side by side, two communities, one of which is made up almost entirely of educated people, while the other is largely composed of illiterate people; and let us further suppose that amongst those considered educated you find that in proportion to their population they have six criminals to where the

more illiterate community have but one; suppose that they have
nearly two paupers to where the more illiterate people have but
one; suppose that they have two insane to where the illiterates have
only one; suppose that their death list shows four suicides to where
that of the illiterates shows but one; and suppose that the same list
shows three deaths from the criminal indulgence of the brutal passions, while that of the illiterates shows but two, what conclusion
would you arrive at with reference to *that kind* of education?

Adhering to the proposition with which we set out a moment
ago, namely, that a people *properly* educated are more moral, virtuous, contented, happy, and law-abiding than an uneducated people, would you not be forced to the conclusion that there must be
something wrong, *terribly*, *radically wrong*, in a system of education so much more direful in its results than even illiteracy itself?

But just here, perhaps, the reader will ask us, as he has a right to
ask, " what application has your supposed case to the question under discussion?" Just have a little patience, good reader, and you
shall see the application.

For this educated community, let us take the native born-white
population of the six New England States, to wit, Massachusetts,
Maine, New Hampshire, Vermont, Connecticut, and Rhode Island,
and for the unlettered community, we will take the native-born
whites of the six States of Virginia, Maryland, Delaware, Georgia,
North Carolina, and South Carolina. It will be observed that the
States thus enumerated are either a part of the original thirteen, or
such as have been carved out therefrom.

Both of these communities started on their career of existence
about the same time; both were composed mainly of people from
the same part of Europe; people who spoke the same language and
had been accustomed to the same laws, manners, and usages; people who possessed the same Christian religion, pretty much all of
whom (outside of little Maryland) were of the protestant faith, and
took as their religious guide the same Bible, and even the same trans-
lation of that Bible.

There was *one* important particular, however, in which these two
communities widely differed at the very start, as we shall presently
see. " More than two hundred years ago the principle was incor-
" porated into the legislation of Massachusetts, that *the whole peo-*
" *ple must* be educated to a certain degree *at the public expense*,
" irrespective of any social distinctions." [1]

---

[1] See work entitled " The Daily Public School," published by J. B. Lippincott in 1866, p. 121.
See Kent's Commentaries, vol. ii, p. 210.

Again : " In Massachusetts, by statute, in 1647 each town consist-
" ing of fifty householders was directed to maintain a school to teach
" their children to read and write, and every town of one hundred
" families was to maintain a grammar school to fit youth for the col-
" lege. The common schools of Massachusetts have been kept up
" to this day by direct tax and individual subscription, and nowhere
" in a population of equal extent has common elementary education
" been more universally diffused."[1]

" The compulsory system of supporting common and grammar
" schools in each town is sustained, to this day, in Massachusetts,
" and enforced by indictment."[2]

At a very early day, after their settlement, a similar system of education was adopted in all the other New England States, from which
fact the system seems to have taken the name of " the New England
" system." Chancellor Kent says : " In New England it has been
" a steady and governing principle from the very foundation of the
" colonies, that it was the right and duty of the government to pro-
" vide, by means of fair and just taxation, for the instruction of all
" the youth in the elements of learning."[3]

On the other hand, the six enumerated States, comprising what we
have agreed to call the unlettered community, steadily resisted the
New England system up to a very recent date.

Virginia, which occupies about the same relation to the latter community that Massachusetts does to the former, according to Lippincott's Gazetteer of the World, published in 1856, had at that time no
general free school system, but " made an appropriation for the instruction of the poor."[4]

Thus these two communities, the one *with* its New England public-school system, and the other *without* it, travelled along, side by
side, for about two hundred years, until A. D. 1860, when the eighth
United States decennial census was taken, and the following was the
showing of these two communities, as will appear by reference to
the annexed table No. 1. We find that at the date referred to, to
wit, 1860, Massachusetts and her five New England sisters had
2,665,945 native-born white inhabitants, and out of these only 8,543
adults who could not read nor write, while Virginia, with her five sisters, numbered 3,181,969 native-born whites, of whom 262,802 adults
could neither read nor write. So that in the six New England States
the proportion of illiterate native whites was only one to every 312,

---

[1] See 2 Kent, 210–211.
[2] Commonwealth *vs.* Inhabitants of Dedham, 16 Mass. R., p. 141.
[3] See 2 Kent, 210.
[4] See Lippincott's " Gazetteer of the World," published in 1856, p. 2049.

while Virginia and her five sisters counted one illiterate to every 12. But mark you! How stand the criminal lists? Massachusetts and her five sisters, out of her native white population of a little more than two and a half millions, had on the first of June, 1860, just 2,459 criminals in prison, while Virginia and her five comparatively unlettered companions, with a native white population of over three millions, had but 477 in prison. That is to say, those educated under the New England system had one native-born white criminal to every 1,084 native white inhabitants, while those who had generally rejected that system had but one prisoner to every 6,670, being a disproportion, according to the whole number of natives whites, of more than six criminals in New England to one in the other community.[1] A glance at the same table will show that the natives educated under the New England system had one pauper to every 178, while those who had managed to live without that luxury had but one pauper to every 345.

Of those who in one year had died by suicide, New England had one to every 13,285 of the entire population, while Virginia and her five sisters had but one suicide to every 56,584, and of those who perished, the victims of their criminal lusts, New England had one to every 84,737, while her neighbors, that had never enjoyed her educational advantages, had but one such victim to every 128,729. We have not before us the list of insane in the several States for 1860, so we borrow from the report furnished by the Census Marshal of 1870, where it appears that the New England system produced (of those born and living in their native States respectively) one insane person to every 800 native-born inhabitants, while the rejection of that system resulted in one insane to 1,682 native inhabitants.[2]

---

[1] Great care has been taken to avoid mistakes in these computations, but should any inaccuracy be discovered, the author will take it as a favor to be informed of the fact, so that it may be corrected in future editions. We omit fractions.

[2] Since the appearance of the first edition of the "Poison Fountain," Prof. Samuel Royce, in a work published in Boston, entitled, "Deterioration and Race Education," although he claims that "the power and wisdom of the State alone are to be trusted with this great work and responsibility" of educating the young, nevertheless admits on pages 462-3, upon the authority of an official report, that there is "*hardly a State or county in the civilized world where atrocious and flagrant crimes are so common as in educated Massachusetts.*" And on page 36, while referring to the alarming increase of crime in America, he says: "*Neither will it answer to lay it to the foreign element, the criminal rate of which has remained the same, or even lessened, while the native criminals have increased during 1860-1870 from 10,143 to 24,173.*"

It is sometimes claimed that the chief reason why the public-school States have so large a proportion of criminals is because of their large cities. It is undoubtedly true that, like every other kind of pestilence, this poisonous and crime-breeding system of education rages with more terrible fury in great cities than in small villages or country places; but that its ravages are by no means confined to large cities is abundantly proved by statistics. For example: In 1860 eleven of Connecticut's largest towns and cities did not equal in population the single city of Baltimore, the metropolis of Maryland, and yet Maryland had but one native white criminal to every 5,276 native white inhabitants; while Connecticut numbered one native white criminal to every 845 inhabitants. At that time Maryland had the public-school system in its infancy, while Connecticut had it in its maturity. But only ten years later, (in 1870,) when Maryland's expenditures for public-school purposes had swollen from $205,319 (the amount expended in 1860) to $1,146,057, her native white criminals had correspondingly increased from one for every 5,276 to one for every 1,717 inhabitants.

TABLE 1—1860.

Showing, 1st, the entire population; 2d, the entire native white population; 3d, the entire number of illiterate native white adults; 4th, the entire number of native white criminals; 5th, paupers; 6th, the entire number of deaths by suicide; 7th, deaths by syphilis in 1860 in the New England States, compared with the six States of Maryland, Virginia, Delaware, Georgia, North Carolina, and South Carolina. For the sources from which these figures are drawn see Eighth U. S. Census Reports for 1860, Mortality and Miscellaneous Statistics, to wit: For total population see page 20; for native white population, page 62; for native illiterates, page 508; for native criminals and paupers, see page 512; for deaths by suicides and from syphilis, pages from 5 to 42.

Results of the Anti-Parental Public School System in 200 Years.

STATES.	Population, total.	Population, native white.	Natives over 21 years of age who can neither read nor write.	Proportion of native illiterate being—	Native criminals in prison June 1st.	Proportion of criminals being—	Native paupers receiving State aid, June 1, 1860.	Proportion of paupers being—	Suicides.	Proportion of suicides being—	Deaths from syphilis.	Proportion being—
Maine	628,279	590,826	2,386	1 to 247	197	1 to 2,999	4,147	1 to 142	33	1 to 19,038	4	1 to 157,069
New Hampshire	326,073	305,135	1,093	" 279	138	" 2,211	2,072	" 147	31	" 10,518	1	" 326,073
Vermont	315,098	282,355	933	" 302	80	" 3,259	1,510	" 186	20	" 15,749		
Massachusetts	1,231,066	970,952	2,004	" 484	1,495	" 649	5,206	" 186	110	" 11,191	26	" 47,348
Connecticut	460,147	379,451	925	" 410	449	" 845	1,548	" 245	28	" 16,433	2	" 230,023
Rhode Island	174,620	137,226	1,202	" 114	100	" 1,372	445	" 308	14	" 12,472	4	" 43,655
Aggregate	3,135,283	2,665,945	8,543	312	2,459	1,064	14,928	178	236	13,285	57	84,737

Results of the Parental System of Education in 200 Years.

STATES.	Population, total.	Population, native white.	Natives over 21 years of age who can neither read nor write.	Proportion of native illiterate being—	Native criminals in prison June 1st.	Proportion of criminals being—	Native paupers receiving State aid, June 1, 1860.	Proportion of paupers being—	Suicides.	Proportion of suicides being—	Deaths from syphilis.	Proportion being—
Maryland	687,049	522,324	33,780	1 to 15	99	1 to 5,276	621	1 to 841	14	1 to 49,074	1	1 to 687,049
Virginia	1,596,318	1,070,395	83,360	" 12	163	" 6,566	4,320	" 247	30	" 53,210	9	" 177,368
Delaware	112,216	101,213	11,563	" 8	19	" 5,329	331	" 305	2	" 56,108		
Georgia	1,057,286	538,417	43,550	" 12	77	" 6,952	1,106	" 486	22	" 48,058	10	" 105,728
North Carolina	992,622	658,264	74,877	" 8	62	" 10,617	1,422	" 462	15	" 66,174	7	" 141,803
South Carolina	703,708	291,316	15,792	" 18	57	" 5,110	1,404	" 207	8	" 87,963	13	" 54,131
Aggregate	5,149,199	3,181,909	262,802	12	477	6,670	9,204	345	91	56,584	40	128,729

Mr. Richard Grant White, of New York, in an article entitled "THE PUBLIC-SCHOOL FAILURE," which appeared in the *North American Review* for December, 1880, quotes extensively from the statistics contained in this pamphlet, and in a foot-note to that article he says: "My attention was directed to these facts by a pamphlet on the system of anti-parental education by the Hon. Zachary Montgomery, of California, which I received on the 23d of October last, after the publication of my articles on the public schools in the *New York Times.* Mr. Montgomery's trenchant pamphlet contains very elaborate tables made up from the United States Census Reports. I have verified them by those reports, and find them essentially accurate and trustworthy."

Table 2—1870.

Showing the number of native-born white criminals, paupers, and insane persons in the six New England States compared with the number of native-born white criminals, paupers, and insane persons in the six neighboring States of Maryland, Virginia—West Virginia included—Delaware, Georgia, North Carolina, and South Carolina. Virginia and West Virginia are counted as one State, in order to include the same territory embraced in table No. 1. This table No. 2, it will be remarked, shows the comparative amount of crime, pauperism, and insanity in the several States enumerated in 1870, after the latter six States had been desolated by a four year's war; after the foundations of their entire social and political fabric had been uprooted, 4,000,000 of negro slaves emancipated, and the reins of most of their State, county, and municipal governments had fallen in the hands of bad negroes, or worse whites; and last, but not least, after the New England anti-parental system of public-school education had taken root in their soil and had begun to produce its natural fruits.

For the figures from which these tables are compiled, see "Compendium of the Ninth Census of the United States," to wit: For entire native population, p. 382; for native white population, p. 383; for native white criminals and paupers, p. 531, and for the insane, born and living in each State, p. 631.

States.	Population, entire native.	Population, native white.	Native white prisoners June 1st.	Proportion of native white prisoners being—	Native white paupers receiving State aid June 1, 1870.	Proportion of native white paupers being	Insane, born and living in the State.	Proportion of insane being—
Maine	578,034	576,097	255	1 to 2,259	3,149	1 to 182	678	1 to 852
New Hampshire	288,689	288,117	199	" 1,447	1,739	" 165	401	" 719
Vermont	283,396	282,492	143	" 1,975	1,231	" 229	357	" 793
Massachusetts	1,104,032	1,090,743	1,152	" 946	5,323	" 204	1,466	" 756
Connecticut	423,815	414,015	215	" 1,925	1,123	" 368	478	" 886
Rhode Island	161,957	156,927	113	" 1,387	407	" 385	189	" 856
Aggregate	2,839,923	2,808,491	2,077	1,352	12,972	216	3,549	800
Maryland	697,482	522,238	304	1 to 1,717	781	1 to 668	497	1 to 1,403
Virginia	1,211,409	698,388	331	" 2,109	1,942	" 358	1,082	" 1,119
Delaware	115,879	93,101	13	" 7,161	223	" 417	47	" 2,465
Georgia	1,172,982	628,173	126	" 4,985	1,270	" 496	508	" 2,305
North Carolina	1,068,332	675,490	132	" 5,117	1,119	" 603	760	" 1,405
South Carolina	697,532	281,894	130	" 2,168	888	" 328	308	" 2,164
West Virginia	424,923	406,951	138	" 2,948	839	" 485		
Aggregate	5,388,539	3,306,235	1,174	2,816	7,062	468	3,202	10,861

TABLE 3.—Compiled from United States Census of 1860. See pages referred to in Table No. 1.

STATES.	Population, total.	Population, native white.	Natives over 21 years who can neither read nor write.	Proportion being one to every—	Native criminals in prison, June 1st.	Proportion being one to every—	Native paupers supported by the State, June 1st, 1860.	Proportion being one to every—	Total suicides.	Proportion being one to every—	Deaths from syphilis.	Proportion being one to every—
Alabama	964,201	516,769	37,302	13	183	2,823	431	1,199	21	45,914	14	68,871
Arkansas	435,450	320,594	23,587	13	61	5,255	175	1,831	3	145,150	1	435,450
California	379,994	233,466	11,509	20	336	694	105	2,223	38	9,999	24	15,883
Connecticut	460,147	379,451	925	410	449	845	1,548	245	28	16,433	2	230,023
Delaware	112,216	101,253	11,503	8	19	5,329	331	305	2	56,108		
Florida	140,424	75,370	5,150	14	13	4,259	105	717	4	35,106	10	105,728
Georgia	1,057,286	538,417	43,550	12	77	6,992	1,106	486	22	48,058	5	342,390
Illinois	1,711,951	1,387,308	39,748	34	313	4,432	707	1,962	44	38,907	4	337,607
Indiana	1,350,428	1,282,244	56,903	22	129	9,552	1,120	1,100	25	54,017	2	337,456
Iowa	674,913	568,682	12,903	44	61	9,325	322	1,766	18	37,495		
Kansas	107,206	94,513	2,695	36	22	4,296	7	13,501	5	21,441	13	88,898
Kentucky	1,155,684	870,402	65,749	13	147	5,921	749	1,162	32	36,115	18	39,333
Louisiana[1]	708,002	293,247	15,679	18	359	816	146	2,008	20	35,400	4	157,069
Maine	628,279	590,826	2,386	247	197	2,999	4,147	142	33	19,038	1	687,049
Maryland	687,049	522,324	33,780	15	99	5,276	621	841	14	49,074	26	47,348
Massachusetts	1,231,066	970,952	2,004	484	1,495	649	5,206	186	110	11,191	3	246,371
Michigan	749,113	600,021	8,170	73	505	1,188	679	883	36	20,808	9	87,922
Mississippi	791,305	346,116	15,136	22	35	9,889	270	1,281	20	39,565	1	1,182,012
Missouri	1,182,012	906,540	51,173	17	166	5,461	513	1,767	29	40,759		
Minnesota	172,023	113,295	1,055	107	16	7,080	39	2,905	4	43,005		
Nebraska	28,841	22,475	357	62	188	2,211	2,072	147	31	10,518	1	826,073
New Hampshire	326,073	305,135	1,093	279	124	4,429	1,308	419	24	28,001	1	672,035
New Jersey	672,035	549,227	12,987	42	2,861	1,007	7,666	375	131	29,623	28	138,597
New York	3,880,735	2,882,095	26,163	110	62	10,617	1,422	462	15	66,174	7	141,803
North Carolina	992,622	658,264	74,877	8	265	7,589	5,700	352	46	50,858	8	292,438
Ohio	2,339,511	2,011,257	48,015	41	6	7,890	15	3,156	1	52,465		
Oregon	52,465	47,343	1,200	39	756	3,274	4,495	550	84	34,597	11	264,201
Pennsylvania	2,906,215	2,475,710	44,930	55	100	1,372	445	308	14	12,472	4	43,655
Rhode Island	174,620	187,226	1,202	114	57	5,110	1,404	207	8	87,963	13	54,131
South Carolina	703,708	291,318	15,792	18	433	1,877	776	1,047	80	36,960	9	123,311
Tennessee	1,109,801	812,856	69,262	11	65	5,818	108	3,502	29	20,835	2	302,107
Texas	604,215	378,227	11,832	31	80	3,529	1,510	186	20	15,749		
Vermont	315,018	289,355	933	302	163	6,566	4,820	247	30	53,210		
Virginia	1,596,218	1,070,305	83,300	12	172	2,900	815	612	18	43,104	9	177,368
Wisconsin	775,881	498,954	2,663	187								

[1] As early as 1850 Louisiana, with an entire native white population of only 293,247, had 664 public or anti-parental schools, 25,046 pupils, with a public-school income of $349,679. Hence the result, in 1850, 1 criminal to every 816.

TABLE 4—1870.   Compiled from United States Census Reports of 1870—same pages as referred to in Table No. 2.

States.	Entire native population.	Native white population.	Nat. white prisoners June 1, 1870.	Relative proportion of native white prisoners in each State being—	Nat. white paup. sup. pub. exp'se June 1, 1870.	Relative proportion of native white paupers in each State being—	Insane born and living in the State.	Relative proportion of insane born and living in each State being—
Alabama	987,030	511,718	149	1 to every 3,434	354	1 to every 1,445	313	1 to every 3,153
Arkansas	479,545	337,230	137	2,607	238	1,240	41	11,693
California	350,416	339,199	662	512	371	936	25	14,016
Connecticut	423,815	424,015	215	1,925	1,123	363	478	886
Delaware	115,879	93,101	13	7,161	223	417	47	2,465
Florida	182,781	91,395	20	4,569	80	1,142	10	18,287
Georgia	1,172,982	628,173	126	4,985	1,270	496	508	2,309
Illinois	2,024,093	1,996,114	1,229	1,624	1,213	1,645	321	6,249
Indiana	1,539,103	1,514,410	691	2,191	2,583	583	604	2,548
Iowa	989,328	933,543	273	3,602	486	2,023	44	22,494
Kansas	316,007	298,041	202	1,473	105	2,848	3	105,335
Kentucky	1,257,613	1,033,346	525	1,972	963	1,075	864	1,455
Louisiana	665,088	301,450	460	635	279	1,080	198	3,358
Maine	578,034	576,097	255	2,259	3,149	182	678	852
Maryland	697,482	522,233	304	1,717	781	668	497	1,403
Massachusetts	1,104,032	1,090,843	1,152	946	5,323	204	1,446	756
Michigan	916,049	900,630	617	1,459	768	1,172	140	6,543
Mississippi	816,731	371,915	128	2,905	413	900	118	6,921
Missouri	1,499,028	1,380,972	893	1,546	1,090	1,266	342	4,383
Minnesota	279,009	277,579	65	4,270	120	2,313	11	25,364
Nebraska	92,245	91,376	35	2,610	54	1,692		
Nevada	23,690	23,332	37	630	27	864		
New Hampshire	288,689	288,117	199	1,447	1,739	165	401	719
New Jersey	717,153	636,589	483	1,421	1,368	501	506	1,417
New York	3,244,406	3,193,160	2,323	1,374	5,289	584	2,612	1,242
North Carolina	1,068,332	675,490	182	5,117	1,119	603	760	1,405
Ohio	2,292,767	2,229,782	892	2,499	2,659	838	1,638	1,399
Oregon	79,323	78,711	55	1,431	62	1,269	4	19,830
Pennsylvania	2,976,642	2,911,750	2,088	1,394	4,354	668	2,451	1,214
Rhode Island	161,957	156,927	113	1,387	407	385	189	856
South Carolina	697,532	281,894	130	2,168	888	328	308	2,264
Tennessee	1,239,204	916,930	342	2,681	966	949	689	1,797
Texas	756,164	501,216	287	2,123	73	6,893	53	14,267
Vermont	283,396	282,492	143	1,975	1,231	229	357	793
Virginia	1,211,409	698,388	331	2,109	1,942	358	1,082	1,119
West Virginia	424,923	406,951	138	2,948	839	485		
Wisconsin	690,171	686,903	192	3,577	374	1,836	46	15,003

TABLE 5—1870.

In 1870, the several States and Territories of the United States, not counting Mississippi, Texas, and Utah, supported 183,198 public-school teachers, educated 6,228,060 public-school pupils, at an expense of $64,030 673. (See Compendium of Ninth Census of the U. S., page 488.) The following table is compiled from the above source :

STATES.	Total number of pupils, male and female, attending the public schools in 1870.	Total income used for public-school purposes.	Cost to every pupil, being—
Alabama	67, 263	$629, 626	$9 36
Arkansas	72, 045	552, 461	7 66
California	75, 527	1, 627, 733	21 55
Connecticut	88, 449	1, 426, 846	16 13
Delaware	16, 835	127, 729	7 58
Florida	10, 132	76, 389	7 53
Georgia	11, 150	175, 844	15 77
Illinois	677, 623	7, 810, 265	11 52
Indiana	446, 066	2, 063, 599	4 62
Iowa	205, 923	3, 245, 352	15 75
Kansas	58, 030	660, 635	11 37
Kentucky	218, 340	1, 150, 457	5 26
Louisiana	25, 832	473, 707	18 33
Maine	152, 765	843, 435	5 52
Maryland	83, 226	1, 146, 057	13 77
Massachusetts	242, 145	3, 207, 826	13 24
Michigan	254, 738	2, 164, 489	8 49
Minnesota	103, 408	895, 204	8 65
Mississippi			
Missouri	320, 313	3, 002, 733	9 65
Nebraska	15, 052	182, 160	12 10
Nevada	1, 856	81, 273	43 78
New Hampshire	59, 408	403, 310	6 78
New Jersey	80, 105	1, 562, 573	19 56
New York	719, 181	8, 912, 024	12 38
North Carolina	41, 912	205, 131	4 89
Ohio	737, 693	8, 528, 145	11 56
Oregon	29, 822	139, 387	4 67
Pennsylvania	745, 734	7, 292, 946	9 77
Rhode Island	27, 250	355, 582	13 04
South Carolina	31, 362	279, 723	8 90
Tennessee	82, 970	683, 008	8 23
Texas			
Vermont	52, 067	516, 702	9 92
Virginia	8, 700	98, 770	11 35
West Virginia	101, 493	599, 811	5 90
Wisconsin	337, 008	2, 209, 384	6 55

One very noticeable fact in this connection, as shown by the fore-going tables, is that in the State of Massachusetts, which claims the honor of being the founder of the New England system of education, while she had by far the smallest porportion of illiterate native-born adults of any, even of the New England States, she had at the same time much the largest proportion of native white criminals, having one criminal to every 649 native white inhabitants.

The nearest approach to her was the showing made by the State of Connecticut, where there was one native white criminal to every 845 native white inhabitants.

And now, good reader; if you will take the pains to turn to the sixth column of figures in table three, which shows the relative pro-portion of native-born white criminals in *every State* in the Union in 1860, you will see that Massachusetts stands solitary and alone in the grand and magnificent proportions of her criminal list. Califor-nia at that time came next to her chosen model, having one native-born white criminal to every 697 native whites, while, as above stated, Massachusetts had one to every 649.

California seems to have resolved, however, not to be surpassed in her crime list even by her great exemplar, for when the next decen-nial census reports were returned, to wit, in 1870, California made a showing of one native white criminal to every 512 native white in-habitants, thus carrying off the palm which ten years before had been awarded to the old State of Massachusetts.

In view of the foregoing facts and figures, is it any wonder that the Boston correspondent of the San Francisco *Morning Call* tells us " that a large number of public-school men have come to the " conclusion that the public-school system of that city is a failure ?"[1] Or is it surprising that another of our leading dailies, the *Alta Califor-nia*, speaking editorially of the same system as it exists in this State, calls it " our anaconda," and declares that if we are to " judge this " system by its apparent fruits, we shall have to pronounce it not " only a melancholy but a most disastrous failure, and that it will " be idle to look for the cause of the general rowdyism, idleness, and " viciousness of the rising generation anywhere but in the training " which it has been receiving ?"[2]

Even after the civil war, which raged with such terrible fury over the Southern and Southwestern States during the years from 1861 to 1865, whereby property to the value of thousands of millions of dollars was destroyed, a servile race was emancipated, and the very

---

[1] See *Morning Call* of August 5, 1877.   [2] *Alta* editorial, January 31, 1872.

foundations of the whole social and political fabric upheaved and broken to atoms—even after all the bad government which bad white men and bad black men had succeeded in forcing upon the subjugated States—still, when the census reports for 1870 were published, they showed that neither their native white criminals nor paupers counted in the proportion even of so much as one to where those counted two who had been for two hundred years subjected to the ravages of the New England public-school system. (See table No. 2.)

And this precious system of education is the great boon for which in 1870 the American people were paying to the tune of $64,030,673,[1] while at the same time they were grinding through this mill of moral death no less than 7,628,060 children. In order to maintain this very same system, California alone expended during the last fiscal year no less than $2,749,729.46, as appears from the recently published biennial report of the State Superintendent of Public Instruction.

Indeed, so infatuated has our young State become with this crime and pauper-breeding system of public instruction, that she has made it a penal offence for the parent or guardian of any child between the ages of 8 and 14 years to keep such child from the public school, even for the sake of sending it to a far better private school of his own choice, and at his own expense, unless he first seeks and obtains the gracious permission of the school directors so to do.

But lest the reader should be disposed to doubt the existence of so tyrannical a statute, here it is as enacted by the California Legislature on the 28th day of March, 1874:

"SECTION 1. Every parent, guardian, or other person in the State of California, having control and charge of any child or children between the ages of 8 and 14 years, shall be required to send any such child or children to a public school for a period of at least two-thirds of the time during which a public school shall be taught in each city and county, or school district, in each school year, commencing on the first day of July, in the year of our Lord one thousand eight hundred and seventy-four, at least twelve weeks of which shall be consecutive, unless such child or children are excused from such attendance by the Board of Education of the city, or city and county, or of the trustees of the school district in which such parents, guardians, or other persons reside, upon its being shown to their satisfaction that his or her bodily or mental condition has been such as to prevent attendance at school, or application to study for the period required, or that the parents or guardians are extremely poor or sick, or that such child or children are taught in a private school or at home in such branches as are usually taught in the primary schools

---

[1] In 1880 the amount was over $96,000,000.

of this State, or have already acquired a good knowledge of such branches ; *Provided*, In case a public school shall not be taught for three months during the year, within one mile by the nearest travelled road of any person within the school district, he shall not be liable to the provisions of this act."

" SECTION 3. In case any parent, guardian, or other person shall fail to comply with the provisions of this act, said parent, guardian, or other person shall be deemed guilty of a misdemeanor, and shall be liable to a fine of not more then twenty dollars ; and for the second and each subsequent offence, the fine shall not be less than twenty dollars nor more than fifty dollars, and the parent, guardian, or other person so convicted shall pay all costs. Each such fine shall be paid to the clerk of the proper Board of Education or of the district trustees."

Thus it is that the votaries of this system have absolutely undertaken, by the most tyrannical legislation, to strip every parent of the guardianship of his children, and to transfer their *entire* control to an irresponsible Board of School Trustees ; so that if these school directors choose to appoint a libertine or a harlot as the tutor of your daughters, and at the same time refuse their gracious permission for you to send them to a private school of your own choice, it is with fines or prison dungeons that the law proposes to reward you, should you, in obedience to the dictates of right, reason, and your own conscience, seek to shield them from the contaminating touch of a vile teacher. Is it any wonder that vice flourishes or that virtue perishes under the influence of such a system?

CHAPTER III.

ANOTHER TEST—DIFFERENCE IN RESULTS BETWEEN A SMALL AND A LARGE DOSE OF ANTI-PARENTAL EDUCATION WHEN OPERATING UPON THE SELF-SAME COMMUNITY.

IN their desperate efforts to find some plausible explanation for the astounding growth of crime in the public-school States, in excess of that found in the parental-school districts, which will vindicate their idolized "*system*," the advocates of State governed schools have sometimes claimed that the difference between the number of convictions for crime in the public-school States and the number found in the parental-school States is owing to a variety of *local* causes, entirely unconnected with and independent of difference in educational systems. But a complete refutation of this assumption is found in the following statistics of public-school education and crime, demonstrating that in the very same localities every material increase of expenditures for public-school purposes has, *without* a single exception, been followed by a corresponding increase of crime. For example:

MASSACHUSETTS.

In 1850 the State of Massachusetts had a native white population of 827,430.[1]

At that date her public-school pupils numbered 176,475, and her income for the support of these schools was $1,006,795, being $5.70 to each pupil.[2]

With this comparatively limited expenditure for the maintainance of her anti-parental schools, she had, out of a native population of 827,430, but 653 native-born criminals, being only one to every 1,267 native inhabitants.

This, comparatively speaking, was a very small number for a public-school State, though a very large number when compared with the number of criminals in any parental or private-school State.

But coming down to 1880, just thirty years later, we find that her income for public-school purposes had swollen to $4,696,612 for the benefit of 316,630 public-school pupils, being $14.83 per pupil, counting every pupil that attended school at any time during the year. But Massachusetts expended on her schools during that same year more than her income, to wit, the sum of $4,720,951, being $20.03 for the pupils in *average* daily attendance.

And out of a native-born white population of 1,320,897 there were 2,070 adult native white convicts,[3] being one to every 638 inhabitants in place of one to every 1,267 as in 1850, and this leaves out of the count some 608 juvenile convicts, confined in various reformatory institutions. By including these, the native white convicts of Massa-

---

[1] See " Compendium of Census for 1870," page 534.

[2] This article was written in 1884, in San Diego, California, and not having the United States Census Reports for 1850 before me, I took from "Lippincott's Gazetteer of the World," (old edition,) both for Massachusetts and Louisiana, the amount expended on their public schools in 1850, and also the number of pupils then being educated in those schools.

The statistics (for 1850) of the other States are taken from the " Compendium of the United States Census of 1870," where they are reproduced from the census of 1850. In this compendium the pupils both of public and private schools are enumerated together, as are also the aggregate expenditures for educational purposes, so that the amounts given, small as they may seem, even exceed the then expenditures for public schools.

Also, at least a small portion of the children enumerated for 1850, even in the States of Connecticut, New Hampshire, Vermont, Massachusetts, Maine, and Rhode Island, were being educated in private schools.

But inasmuch as there was far more virtue in those States in 1850 than in 1880, it is not probable that the friends of *the system* will complain of a failure to credit any of said pupils to private schools.—EDITOR.

[3] See " Compendium United States Census for 1880," pages 332, 1638–39.

chusetts, in 1880, would amount to one out of every 493 native white inhabitants.

CONNECTICUT.

Turning now to Connecticut, " the land of steady habits," we find an entirely similar condition of things. In 1850 Connecticut had in her schools 79,003 pupils, with an income for school purposes of $430,826, being $5.45 per pupil. At that time her native population[1] numbered 331,560, of whom 244 were convicts, being one to every 1,358 native inhabitants.

But in 1880[2] her income for public schools was $1,441,255, being $12.15 for every pupil that attended at any time during the year; or, counting only the 72,725 pupils in average daily attendance, it would be $19.81 per pupil, and out of a native white population of 481,060 she had 432 adult criminals, being one to every 1,136, leaving out of the count 403 juvenile convicts, the most damaging portion of the whole record, which, when added to the adults, makes 835 criminals, or one to every 576 native whites.[3]

VERMONT.

Likewise in 1850 Vermont had an income for school purposes of $246,604 for the education of 100,785 pupils,[4] being $2.44 per pupil. At that time she had a native population of 280,055, of whom only 64 or one to every 4,372, were criminals. But turning to the census report for 1880, we find her expending $452,693 upon 73,237 pupils, being $6.31 per pupil, or counting only the 47,206 pupils in average daily attendance and we have $9.58 per pupil. And instead of one criminal to every 4,372 inhabitants, as in 1850, she had out of a native white population of 290,281 just 196 adult native convicts, being one to every 1,481 native whites. When to these are added 134 native white juvenile offenders, of whom she seems to have had none in 1850, we shall have an aggregate of 330, or one native white criminal to every 879 native whites.

---

[1] See " United States Compendium Census for 1870," page 534. The report before me for 1850 makes no separate classification of the whole number of native whites and native blacks in the free States.—EDITOR.

[2] See Census for 1880.

[3] The United States Commissioner of Education in his report for 1881, pages 686 to 691, enumerates 71 reformatory institutions in the United States. Only six of these were in existence in 1850, to wit, two in Massachusetts, three in New York, and one in Philadelphia, so that it is taken for granted that prior to that time children in Connecticut were either less addicted to crime than at present, or else they were sent to prison like other criminals, and were consequently included in the enumeration of criminals.

[4] See " Compendium United States Census Reports for 1870," p. 492.

NEW HAMPSHIRE.

New Hampshire, in 1850, expended on her schools, public and private, the sum of $221,146 for the education of 81,237 pupils, being $2.72 per pupil, and at that time, out of a native population of 303,563, she had just 25 native criminals, being one to every 12,142. But thirty years later we find her with an income of $559,-133 for the use of 64,670 pupils, being $8.64 for every pupil attending school at any time during the year, or $11.42 per pupil if we only count the 48,943 in average daily attendance, and, *presto, change*, instead of one native criminal to every 12,142 as in 1850, when expending about one-fourth as much for each pupil, she has out of 299,995 natives 209 native white criminals, or one to every 1,435 native white inhabitants. If to these be added New Hampshire's native white juvenile criminals for 1880, to wit, 91, we shall have an aggregate of 300, or one to every 999 of her native white population.

MAINE.

In 1850 Maine's total expenditures for schools, public and private, was $380,623 for the education of 199,745 pupils, being $1.90 per pupil, and at that time, out of a native population of 550,878, she had but 66 native criminals, being one to every 8,346 native inhabitants.

But in 1880 her income for public schools reached the sum of $1,074,554, for the use of 150,811, being $7.11 for every pupil that attended school at any time during the year, or if we count only the 106,760 in average daily attendance we shall have $10.00 per pupil; and out of a native white population of 588,193 she had 321 adult native white criminals, being one to every 1,832, and if we add her 112 native white juvenile criminals we shall have 433, or one to every 1,358.

RHODE ISLAND.

Rhode Island, in 1850, expended on all her schools $136,729 for the benefit of 24,881 pupils, being $5.53 per pupil, and out of a native population of 123,564 she had 58 criminals, being one to every 2,130. But in 1880 her public-school income was $541,810 for the benefit of 42,489 pupils, being $12.74 for every pupil that attended school at any time during the year, or if we only count the 27,453 in average daily attendance, we should have $19.73 per pupil, and out of a native white population of 196,108 she had 187 native white adult criminals, being one to every 1,049 native white inhabitants. Add to these her 141 native white juvenile offenders, and we have 328, or one to every 597.

This completes the circuit of the six New England States where the system originated, where it has longest existed, and its results have been the most thoroughly tested.

LOUISIANA.

Of all the States of the Union, Louisiana, thirty years ago, was the most lavish in the expenditures of her money for public or anti-parental school purposes.   According to "Lippincott's Gazetteer of the World," (see old edition, p. 1091,) Louisiana had, in 1850, 664 public schools with 25,046 pupils, and $349,679 income for public-school purposes.   The amount would be $13.96 per pupil for every child attending the public schools, which was more than double the amount at that time being paid even by any of the New England States, and the result was already cropping out in her criminal statistics, for during this same year the United States Census Reports show that out of a native white population of 186,577 she had 240 native criminals, being one to every 777, by far the largest criminal record in proportion to population at that time to be found anywhere in America, if not in the world.

Still, *in order to prevent crime*, she continued to increase her expenditures for public-school purposes, until in 1870 she was expending $473,000 on 25,832 pupils, amounting to $18.33 per pupil ; and the result was, that out of a native white population of 301,450 she had 460 native white criminals, being one to every 655 native white inhabitants.

But coming down to 1880, Louisiana—according to the census reports of that year—out of a native white population of 402,177, had but 89 native white convicts in prison, being but one to every 4,518.

Lest some enthusiastic admirer of our great and glorious *system*, in a desperate effort to find *one* supporting fact for his tottering idol, should jump to the conclusion that this great falling off in Louisiana's catalogue of criminals, between 1850 and 1880, was owing to her increased *anti-parental education* facilities, let us caution him to first glance at her educational statistics for that year. From these statistics he will learn that Louisiana's public-school income was but $498,409 for the benefit of 81,012 public-school children, being only $6.15 per pupil ; or counting only those in daily average attendance, it would be still only $8.93 per pupil, in lieu of the $18.33 per pupil in 1870.

NEW YORK.

In 1850 the State of New York had a native-born population of 2,436,771. She then had in her schools, all told, 727,156 pupils, at an annual cost of $2,431,247, or $3.34 per pupil. At that time her native-born criminals numbered only 649, or one native-born criminal to every 3,754 native inhabitants.

But with the laudable purpose of lessening the tendency of her people to commit crime, the State government went on year by year increasing the burdens of taxation for public-school purposes, until in 1880 her receipts for the education of 1,027,938 children were $11,035,511, being $10.78 for every pupil that entered her schools at any time during the year, and the result was that, with a native white population of 3,807,317, she had 5,177 native white criminals in prison, being one to every 741 people, instead of one to every 3,754 as in 1850. That is to say, having increased her expenditures for anti-parental and godless schools a little more than *three hundred per cent.* in order to DECREASE crime, she was rewarded by an *increase* of crime to the tune of over *five hundred* per cent.

What seems astonishing is that, in the face of these appalling facts, the demand for more money, more money, still goes forth from those who have grown rich by the ruin of the rising generation. We shall here extract from the report of the United States Commissioner of Education for 1881 (page 71) the following refreshing piece of information.

Referring to New York's State Superintendent as his authority the Commissioner says :

"With an increase of nearly 21,000 in the number of youth, five to twenty-one years of age, there was a decrease of over 10,000 in public-school enrolment, and over 13,000 in average daily attendance. * * * He thinks the schools increased in efficiency in greater proportion than the attendance fell off, and that the results attained justified the expenditure, which was $511,026 greater than the preceding year. * * * The figures show a smaller number of public-school houses, but a greater estimated value of school property, 28,000 fewer volumes in district libraries, an average school term of one day shorter, fewer men and more women teaching, but a slight increase in their average pay."

Here is certainly some valuable food for reflection for such as have stomachs sufficiently strong to digest it. From this statement it would appear that the *cost* of public-school work in the State of New York increases in an *inverse* ratio to the number of pupils taught, while, as we have seen, *crime increases in direct proportion to such cost.*

But, says the Superintendent, " the schools increased in *efficiency* in *greater* proportion than the attendance fell off." And the only evidence he furnishes us in corroboration of this statement is found in the fact that 28,000 *volumes disappeared from the district libraries* in the short period of one school year. History tells us that in ancient Sparta the most accomplished and highly honored youths were those who could steal without being caught. But we very much doubt if Sparta's lads in her palmiest days could have purloined 28,000 books in so short a time and escaped detection.

OHIO.

In 1850 Ohio had a native population of 1,757,746, and was expending on 502,826 pupils $1,018,258, or $2.02 per pupil, and at that time she had but 102 native-born criminals, being one native criminal to every 17,232 people. But in 1880 she was receiving from the people $11,085,315 for the public-school education of 752,944 pupils, being $14.72 per pupil, and out of a native white population of 2,723,582 she had 1,674 criminals, being one to every 1,626, in place of one to every 17,232 as in 1850. In other words, while Ohio was increasing her expenditures upwards of *sevenfold* in order to check crime, her criminals increased upwards of *tenfold*.

(See United States Census Report for 1880.)

ILLINOIS.

Take, again, the State of Illinois. In 1850 that State was expending on 130,411 pupils $403,138, or $3.08 per pupil. And out of a native population of 736,149 she had 164 criminals, being one to every 4,488. But she went on increasing her godless educational fund until in 1880 she was expending, on 704,041 children, $9.850,011, being $13.99 per pupil ; and out of a native white population of 2,448,172 she had 2,223 native-born white criminals, or one to every 1,101. To put the case in words instead of figures, it may be stated thus :

In order to prevent crime and thus protect the property, the lives, the liberties, and the reputations of her citizens, Illinois, in the space of thirty years, more than quadrupled her annual expenditures *per capita* for the anti-parental education of her pupils, and the result was that she more *than quadrupled the ratio of her native-born white criminals to prey upon her people.*

We cannot, in the short space of one article, review the history of education and crime in all the States, but we must not close without a brief allusion to our own California.

In 1860 California had in her public schools 24,977 pupils, with an income for public-school purposes of $353,096, being $14.13 for each pupil. Her record of crime amongst her native-born whites at that time surpassed everything in the United States except that of Massachusetts. She then had out of a native white population of 233,466, some 336 native white convicts, being one to every 694. But in 1880 California collected an income of $3,525,520 for the use of 161,477 pupils, being $21.83 apiece for each pupil that ever darkened the door of a public-school house at any time during the year, or $33.20 each for the 106,179 in average daily attendance, and she had a corresponding crop of adult native white criminals of 1,396 out of a native white population of 549,529, being one to every 393 of her native white population. And if to these we add her 142 native white youths serving their time in reformatories, we shall have one native white criminal to every 357 native white inhabitants.

In conclusion let us take a bird's eye view of this question of anti-parental education and crime, as it affected the whole country at the two periods above-named, to wit, in 1850 and in 1880.

In 1850, our income in the whole United States for our public and private schools was $16,162,000. The whole number of pupils in both classes of schools at that time was 3,642,694, consequently our expenditures for educational purposes were $4.40 per pupil. At that time our native white population numbered some 17,308,460, and our native white criminals 4,326, or one to every 4,001 of the native white population (omitting fractions.)

But in 1880 our public school income alone reached the enormous sum of $96,857,534,[1] being $9.72 per pupil for each of the 9,946,-160 pupils who at any time during the year entered a public-school house; or, counting only the 6,276,398 in average daily attendance, and we have $15.43 per pupil. And during that year (1880) out of a native white population of 36,843,291 we had 29,377[2] native white criminals, making one criminal for every 1,254 inhabitants, instead of one to every 4,001 as in 1850. If to the above number, 29,377 native white adult convicts, we add the 9,118 native white juvenile convicts in our seventy-one reformatory institutions, we shall have 38,495, or one to every 957 native white people.

Should any mistake in any of our figures be discovered, we shall be obliged to the person making such discovery to inform us of the

---

[1] This is independent of expenses of State officers of public instruction, normal schools, colleges, and schools for Indian children.
[2] The whole number of native convicts as given in the Census Reports for 1880 was 46,338, 16,961 of whom were colored. Deducting these leaves the number above given.

fact, as we have no desire to perpetrate an injustice, even against as great an enemy of our race as we believe our anti-parental public-school system to be.

We here take occasion to caution the reader—as we have done before—against drawing from our figures or our arguments any inference that we look upon education as the cause of crime. On the contrary, we maintain that ignorance is the mother of vice. But it is against a *false system* of education that we are leveling our batteries—a system that intrusts to politicians an authority over the child which can only be properly wielded by its own parents.

In the face of these startling statistics, is it not high time for those who claim that the present public-school system tends to *diminish* crime, to point out at least *one* State or *one fraction* of a State where the system has *not produced exactly the opposite result ?*

Our figures are official, and if any friend of our present public-school system will take them, read them, study them, and from them or any other reliable authority prove that the present public-school system tends to *prevent crime*, he will perform a more stupendous miracle than if he should raise the dead to life.

A DIALOGUE WITH A MORAL UNDERSTOOD.

Madam JONATHAN, whose son, young JONATHAN, lies at death's door from a *tumor*, consults Dr. PLAIN TALK.

Madam JONATHAN. " Oh, Dr., what shall I do ?"

Dr. PLAIN TALK. " Well, madam, what's the matter now ?"

Madam JONATHAN. " Oh, Dr., my poor, *poor* boy Jonathan Junior had a mite of a tumor, the size of a pea, you know, and we called in Dr. PUFFUMBIG, and Dr. PUFFUMBIG said : ' Give the boy, every day, an ounce of some sort of stuff he called ' *common skules*,' just to purify the blood and dry up the tumor, you know. And I gave it to Jonathan Junior, and in a week's time the tumor was as big as a hen's egg. And Dr. PUFFUMBIG said, ' Double the dose of *common skules*.' And I doubled it. And in another week the tumor was as big as your head, Dr. And Dr. PUFFUMBIG said it was all because I was too pleggy stingy with the ' *common skules*.' ' Give him at *least a pound of common skules* three times a day,' said Dr. PUFFUMBIG. And, fool like, I gave it, and now that ugly tumor is as big as a milk-pail. Oh, Dr., what shall I do ?"

Dr. PLAIN TALK. " Well, madam, if it is your desire to turn your boy *all into tumor* I must say you have the right doctor, and he has prescribed the right treatment. In fact, I think you might ransack the apothecaries of the infernal regions without finding anything better suited to such a purpose. And, pray, what is your own opinion, madam ?"

Madam JONATHAN (pensively). " I guess it's a mighty nice thing for Dr. PUFFUMBIG, who sells his nasty stuff for $96,000,000 at a dash, but a horrid thing for my *poor Jonathan* Senior and *Jonathan Junior, too*, since the one has to foot these monstrous bills, while the other is dying of the tumor made an awful sight worse by the dirty *pizen* of that unmitigated old quack."

CHAPTER IV.

YET ANOTHER STARTLING TEST—A VOICE FROM THE GRAVE OF THE SUICIDE.

THE gratuitous and utterly unsupported assertion has sometimes been made by the friends of State-controlled education that the reason why statistics show the largest list of criminals in those localities where the most money has been lavished upon the public schools is because those are the only localities where the criminals are all, or nearly all, caught and convicted; while in those places where there is little or no public-school training the criminals cannot be caught.

Now it will scarcely be denied that *dead* criminals CAN be caught even in those States where they have no public schools.

Then how stands the record with reference to this particular class of criminals?

As we have already seen, it was in the early period of their first settlement in America that the colonists of Massachusetts, Maine, Connecticut, New Hampshire, Vermont, and Rhode Island tried the experiment of taking from the fathers and mothers the educational control of their own children and entrusting it to the general public, while six other colonies, to wit, Maryland, Virginia, Delaware, Georgia, North Carolina, and South Carolina left this educational control of children in the hands of parents, their natural guardians. With slight exceptions, in a few of the last-named communities, (towards the close of the period,) this experiment continued down to 1860.

The comparative number of suicides in these two localities, as shown by the United States Census Reports for that year, was as follows. (See tables *ante.*)

WHERE THE STATE CONTROLLED EDUCATION—SUICIDES.	WHERE THE PARENTS CONTROLLED EDUCATION—SUICIDES.
Maine.................................to every 19,738	Maryland...........................1 to every 49,074
New Hampshire....................1 to every 10,518	Virginia.............................1 to every 53,210
Vermont.........................1 to every 15,749	Delaware............................1 to every 56,108
Massachusetts......................1 to every 11,191	Georgia.............................1 to every 48,058
Connecticut...... ....1 to every 16,433	North Carolina....................1 to every 66,074
Rhode Island........................1 to every 12,472	South Carolina ....1 to every 87,963
Aggregate........ ....1 to every 13,285	Aggregate.......... ....1 to every 56,584

An analysis of these figures will show that in every solitary instance where the political State had controlled the education and training of children, the ratio of suicides ranged from 250 per cent. to 800 per cent. higher than where the education and training had been left to parental control, while the aggregate ratio shows over four times as many suicides under *State* education as under parental education. This enormous excess in the number of suicides amongst people educated under *State* control over that found amongst those educated under parental control *must* have a *cause*, and a cause adequate to the effect. Now,

WHAT IS THE CAUSE?

In explanation of the facts shown by the foregoing statistics, we maintain that there are chiefly two causes, both of which are intimately connected, the one, in fact, springing from the other. The first cause which we propose to consider is the loss of parental authority and home influence over children, through and by means of a State-controlled system of education. The second cause, and one which, as just stated, is closely allied to the first, is a neglect of moral and religious education and training.

It requires little argument to prove either to the readers of history, or to the close observer of current events, or to any affectionate son or daughter, who has grown to manhood or womanhood under the guardianship of an intelligent, affectionate, and conscientious father and mother, that parental influence is one of the Almighty's chief agencies for promoting the purity, preservation, and happiness of the human race. All history, all philosophy, and all poetry point to the home as the birthplace and nursery of virtue, morality, patriotism, and religion. Home is the ever-living fountain of present joys, sweet memories, and cherished hopes. Where is the little lad or lass whose heart does not gladden, whose eye does not brighten, and whose pace does not quicken while returning from field or forest or school, when nearing the loved spot which he or she calls by the sacred name of home? What colors can paint, or what words describe, the sweet pleasures of a truly happy home?

What artist has ever yet delineated the matchless charms of the true conjugal and maternal love that beams in the eye, dimples the cheek, or quivers in the voice of the true wife and mother, radiating, illuminating, and cheering the home and sending sunshine and warmth, and life and hope and happiness into the hearts and souls of husband and sons and daughters and friends? Or where on earth can there be found a truer picture of the primeval paradise than in an intelligent, virtuous, orderly, affectionate, united, and happy family of father, mother, and children? He who enjoys such a home, or the cheering hope of such a home, or even the bright and soothing memory of such a home, will find therein an ever-present talisman, an almost infallible shield against the horrible crime of self-destruction. Who, in his sane mind and sober senses, can ever seriously plot against his own life, however burdensome that life may have become, when remembering that in doing so he is plotting against the happiness of brothers and sisters to whom he is bound by the endearing ties of blood and ten thousand sweet memories; against an aged father and mother whom he loves, and by whom he is beloved with an ardor that knows no cooling; against the devoted and faithful wife of his bosom, and against his own helpless, innocent, and confiding babes?

These considerations are, however, in one sense, only collateral barriers against the crime of self-murder, and, unless supported by higher and stronger motives, are liable to be battered down by the surging billows of human passion, or to be crushed by the almost unbearable weight of worldly woes.

But a deeper and stronger barrier against this black and horrid crime is found in an educated conscience.

In marshaling our proofs in support of this proposition, we shall assert:

First, That man is a rational creature, and, being rational, whatever he does while possessed of his reason he does for a motive. The motive may be a good one or it may be a bad one, but it is, nevertheless, a motive.

Secondly, Above all other considerations personal to himself, man naturally hates misery and loves happiness. Hence, whatever he does or refuses to do while in the exercise of his reason, is done, or refused to be done, for the purpose of avoiding misery or of finding happiness.

Thirdly. Men differ widely as to their choice of roads in the pursuit of happiness, as well as in their efforts to avoid misery; and,

Fourthly. There are chiefly three roads by which men travel in their pursuit of happiness or in their flight from misery, namely: (1) The road which leads to the gratification of the animal appetites, and which avoids whatever tends to their restraint; (2) the road which leads to human applause and worldly honors, while keeping at a distance from whatever wounds pride or vanity; (3) the road which leads to truth and justice; to the triumph of God Almighty's

law ; to honors imperishable ; and to happiness unmixed with pain
and as enduring as eternity itself. Unlike the other roads, this
turns neither to the right nor to the left ; neither to shun that which
pains the body or mortifies vanity or pride. Its course is ever up-
ward and onward. The truly faithful traveller upon this road,
instead of repining at the endurance of bodily pain, the loss of fortune, the betrayal of friends or the malice of enemies, seizes upon
those passing woes as so many precious coins with which to purchase imperishable joys.

Now, it requires but a moment's reflection to enable us to see
that a man's choice, as between these three roads, must, in the nature of things, depend very much on his early training and education.

Man has three classes of faculties, namely : the faculties of the
body, the faculties of the mind, and the faculties of the conscience ;
and, undoubtedly, all these three classes of faculties were designed
by the Creator to be exercised, and to be exercised in harmony.
But, in order to be exercised in harmony, it is necessary, in the nature of things, either that the demands of these three faculties be
always in harmony, or else, in cases of conflict, one class of desires
must yield obedience to another class. But it is easy to see that
these three classes of desires are *not* always in harmony, for it often
happens that one class of desires—as, for example, in the case of an
inordinate desire for strong drink or impure pleasures—are directly
at war both with the desires of the mind and the conscience, and it
can scarcely require argument to prove that, in such cases of conflict, the desires of the body ought to yield obedience to the opposing
desires of mind and conscience. But then, again, the mind may,
and often does, in defiance of conscience, at the peril of bodily health
and life, and even at the hazard of disaster to itself, desire to circum-
vent, overreach, defraud, and ruin others, and would, in its vaulting
ambition, go so far as to usurp the throne of God Himself. Hence,
in all cases of conflict between the unjust desires of mind and the
dictates of conscience, the conscience should rule supreme. And,
unless conscience do rule supreme, there is no adequate barrier to
check the wrongs which the body and mind may perpetrate against
themselves, against each other, against conscience, or against God
and society. Hence, the true welfare, the safety and the happiness
of every man's body, mind and conscience, as well as the safety of
society, demand that every man's conscience should reign supreme
over both his bodily appetites and his mental desires, aims, and
ambitions. But all these three classes of man's faculties need edu-

cation, training, and exercise. The physical man needs education, training, and exercise, not only to give him bodily strength and skill, but to teach and accustom him to subject his animal appetites to the dictates of mind and conscience. The mind needs to be taught and trained and exercised, not only to strengthen and store it with knowledge necessary for the proper direction and government of the body, and the enlightenment of itself and of conscience by the lamp of reason, but to accustom it to habits of prompt and willing obedience to conscience. And the conscience needs to be educated, trained, and exercised, in order that it may learn and accustom itself to walk always in the path whither duty calls and to which right reason points, and never to allow either itself or its mind or its body to stray from that path. But, while it is true that the entire man, including body, mind, and conscience, requires education, training, and exercise, it is no less true that the conscience, the governing part of man, most of all requires this education, training, and exercise.

If an individual in the private walks of life makes a mistake for the want of proper education or training, the evil consequences of such a mistake are usually unfelt by the general public, but if the governor of a State, or the President of the United States, for a similar reason, make a mistake in his official capacity, then the whole country must suffer the consequences. So, likewise, if, for the want of proper bodily training, a boy stumps his toe or cuts his finger, while his body must endure a temporary pain, yet his mind is not impaired nor his conscience tarnished. So, if for want of mental education, the boy should insist that the world is flat instead of round, or should prove himself so deficient in a knowledge of figures as to lose his situation, he might still escape the pangs of a guilty conscience and preserve a spotless reputation for integrity. But if, for the want of a conscience, educated, trained, exercised, and strengthened in habits of honesty, he should pocket his employer's money, in obedience to the demands of his animal appetite or to satisfy the claims of vanity, the whole man would suffer. For example: the conscience would suffer not only from remorse, but it would suffer from being blunted and obscured, and rendered less fit to perform its functions; the mind would suffer from anxiety and the fear of discovery, or from the mortification of detection; and the body would suffer from the labor required to cover the tracks of guilt, or from being forced to endure the punishment which either the natural or the human law, or both, would visit upon it. Can it, then, be denied that the education, training, and constant exercise of the conscience is of the very

first and greatest importance in giving direction and formation
to the human character? Of course we are now addressing ourselves to those who recognize the existence of the human conscience as the great director and regulator of human motives and
human actions. Ought, then, the consciences of children to be
developed, instructed, and exercised as a part of their education?
And ought this instruction and education to go hand in hand with
the education and training of the mind and body during the hours
of school?

It is maintained by multitudes of parents and many clergymen,
while admitting that it is necessary that the consciences of children
should be educated, that this education ought to be confined to the
home circle and the church, and that the daily school should be
exclusively reserved for the education of the mind and the body.
But have we not seen that the conscience must be the governor
and supreme ruler of the entire man ; that the conscience must be
taught the habit of governing, and that both the mind and body
must be taught habits of prompt and willing obedience? But if,
throughout the live-long day, the conscience is to remain practically
dormant, while the mind and body are both in the process of active
development, what will be the necessary result?

Is it not a universally admitted fact that every human organ,
whether it be an organ of the body, the mind, or the conscience, is
strengthened by exercise and weakened by disuse? Then, how is
it possible that the conscience can maintain its supremacy over the
mind and body if it is to be left sleeping or chained down in mute
and motionless bondage, while the body and mind are daily growing in strength, activity, and habits of insubordination? If, from
the cradle to the grave, there is any one period of life more than
any other when the conscience not only needs to be trained, but to
be called into active service, it is during the time spent at school.
It is then that pride and vanity, and anger and lust, and all the
other passions that war against conscience are in their most active
state of development; and if, instead of training these growing passions in habits of subjection to conscience, and instead of training
the conscience to the habit of wielding its authority over these passions, the passions, on the contrary, be trained to lord it over the conscience, what must be the natural result? When a child has reached
manhood, with passions fully developed and trained to command,
and a conscience dwarfed and enfeebled by disuse, and trained to
habits of base and cowardly servitude, what power, short of a miracle,
can sufficiently restore the lost energy of such a conscience or give it

the mastery over the entire man? But when the conscience has lost her sceptre and become the slave of the mere animal or intellectual man, then such a man lives only for the present life, and looks not beyond the portals of the grave, either in his search for happiness or in his flight from pain. Such a man seeks happiness, chiefly, either in the gratification of his animal appetites, or in the acquisition of wealth, or in the paths of wordly ambition, marching to the music of human applause and grasping at the bubble of fame. So long as an average success continues to crown the efforts of one of these seekers after mere worldly happiness, the chances are that he will consent to live ; but let disaster overtake him, and what then? If a man of wealth, let fires, or floods, or a touch of hard times sweep away his accumulated millions ; if an over-ambitious man, let the last lingering hope of political preferment be blasted ; or if he be a man enchained in the bondage of his unholy lusts, let even the crime-steeped partner of his debaucheries frown cruelly upon him, and what assurance have we that he will not cut short the miserable existence that has ceased to yield pleasure and promises nothing but disappointment and pain?

The man who suffers from a raging tooth-ache is not censured for swallowing a small dose of laudanum in the hope of putting himself to sleep until the period of pain shall have passed ; and if death were an eternal sleep and life promised nothing but pain, who could be censured if, to escape a life of suffering or shame, he should so enlarge his dose of laudanum as to render his sleep perpetual?

Here, then, in our humble opinion, is the true source of that alarming growth of suicides so prevalent in the United States. It is found in an educational system which has broken down parental authority, sundered the sacred bonds of affection that bound together brothers and sisters, parents and children, and which has weakened and almost obliterated the human conscience.

It requires but a moment's reflection to show that the same causes which lead to the crime of suicide lead to every other crime known to the laws of God or man. Both reason and daily experience prove that the man or woman who has no sweet and endearing memories of childhood's home ; who cherishes no love for father or mother or brother or sister ; and, worse still, the man or woman who believes in no God, no devil, no heaven, no hell, can never be trusted. Such a man may reach the very pinnacle of wealth and fame and political power ; he may be flattered and praised and applauded by the press and the people as the very pink of patriotism and honesty ; but let the day of trial of come ; let the voice of duty call to the right, while his ruling passion for guilty pleasure, forbidden wealth, or crime-bought fame beckons to the left; and duty may call, and call, and call; but, alas! it will call in vain.

CHAPTER V.

MR. WINES, SPECIAL CENSUS AGENT, ON THE FEARFUL INCREASE OF OUR
INSANE, IDIOTIC, BLIND, AND DEAF-MUTES.

MR. FRED. H. WINES, Special Census Agent, in his preface to the statistics of crime, pauperism, insanity, etc., for 1880, presents the following synopsis of the number of the insane, idiots, blind, and deaf-mutes found in the United States during the years 1880, 1870, 1860, and 1850, respectively, to wit:

CLASS.	1880.	1870.	1860.	1850.
Insane	91,997	37,432	24,042	15,610
Idiots	76,895	24,527	18,930	15,787
Blind	48,928	20,320	12,658	9,794
Deaf-mutes	33,878	16,205	12,821	9,803
Totals	251,698	98,484	68,451	50,994

As remarked by the Agent, the total population for each of these years was as follows, to wit:

"In 1850 it was 23,191,876; in 1860, 31,443,321; in 1870, 38,558,-371; and in 1880 it was 50,155,783. In other words, while the population has only a little more than doubled in thirty years, the number of defective persons returned is nearly five times as great as it was thirty years ago.

"During the past decade (or since 1870) the increase in population has been thirty per cent.; but the apparent increase in the defective classes has been a little more than one hundred and fifty-five per cent."

As shown elsewhere, it is also painfully apparent that our criminals have increased almost in the exact ratio with the increase of our insane, idiotic, and other defective classes.

In commenting on the astounding growth of crime, insanity, pauperism, etc., in the United States during the last thirty years, the Special Agent says:

" The interest and importance of the inquiry into the number and condition of the defective classes, and of the criminal and pauper population, arises from the fact that these are burdens to be borne— drains upon the vitality of the community. When we consider the growth of our population and our material resources, we are in danger of forgetting that there is another side to the picture. It is startling to know that of 50,000,000 of inhabitants over 400,- 000 are either insane, idiots, deaf-mutes, or blind, or inmates of prisons, reformatories, or poor-houses. If to these we add the out- door poor and the inmates of private charitable institutions, the num- ber will swell to nearly or quite half a million, or one per cent. of the total population."

We italicize and fully indorse the closing words of the Agent, in which he says:

" *We cannot begin too soon or prosecute too vigorously the in- quiry into the causes of the prevalence of these evils, which are like a canker at the heart of all our prosperity. Nothing can be more important than for us to ascertain, at the earliest possible moment, the rate at which they are increasing and the means of arresting their growth.*

" The subject is obscure," says the Agent, " *but in the study of it we may almost be said to have our finger upon the pulse of the nation.*"

While, as suggested, we fully indorse the said italicized words. we are not entirely disposed to indorse the declaration that the sub- ject is an " obscure" one, especially to those who will carefully ex- amine the statistics embodied in his report, and study them by the light of a few common-sense principles.

If it is true that a child *brought up in the way he should go will not depart from it when he is old*, who will venture to deny that there has been something radically wrong in the bringing up of a generation which so readily and so rapidly betakes itself to the paths of crime, or which, either ignorantly or otherwise, brings upon itself the constantly increasing maladies of idiocy, insanity, and kindred evils?

In 1880 our public-school property was valued at $211,411,540. Our receipts during that one year for public-school purposes reached the enormous sum of $96,857,534. There were gathered into our public schools 9,946,160 children, and out of our public-school treas- ury we were paying $55,745,029, in the way of salaries, to some 236,019 public-school teachers, in order to prevent crime and save the expenses of paying peace-officers and building city prisons, county jails, and State penitentiaries. And behold the result!!

Our towns and cities swarm with policemen ; our prisons, workhouses, and reformatories are crowded almost to suffocation with impecunious thieves, robbers, and cut-throats, while gilded crime goes unpunished, and moneyed malefactors without number strut our streets with heads erect, spit upon the law, laugh justice to scorn, and fatten upon their ill-gotten millions, while multitudes of their wronged and ruined victims are lodged in almshouses and lunatic asylums, or seek refuge from so sad a fate in the still more horrid doom of self-destruction.

CHAPTER VI.

POLITICAL POISON IN THE PUBLIC-SCHOOL BOOKS—TEN MILLIONS OF AMER-
ICAN CHILDREN FORCED TO DRINK DAILY THE DEADLY DOCTRINE OF
CENTRALIZATION AND DESPOTISM!!!

From a Speech by the Author, delivered at San Diego, Cal., Oct. 30, 1884.

IN our California public schools, as in those of most of the other States, Webster's Dictionary is the legally established authority for the definition of words. This would all be well enough if the Webster of to-day were the Webster of twenty-five years ago. But the illustrious and patriotic Noah Webster would blush in his grave at the thought of being made to father the bastard brood of political heresies which are now being taught in our public schools, through the medium of a false, forged, and mutilated dictionary bearing his honored name.

To show how the overthrow of constitutional liberty and the inestimable right of democratic self-government are being brought about by changing the meaning of words, a few examples will suffice.

Take for example the word " Constitution." " Webster's Una-bridged Dictionary," as published in 1859, in giving the legal defi-nition of the word " Constitution," says :

" In free States the Constitution is paramount to the statutes or laws enacted by the Legislature, limiting and controlling its power; and in the United States the Legislature is created and its powers designated by the Constitution."

But every word of the above definition is expunged from the Webster now used and required by law to be used in our public schools, and in its place we find the following definition of the word " Constitution," to wit:

" The principal or fundamental laws which govern a State or other organized body of men, and are embodied in written documents or implied in the institutions or usages of the country or society."

Thus, under public-school tuition, the rising generation no longer look upon the written Constitution as the source and limit of legislative power; but on the contrary the mere *" usages of society "* are raised to the dignity of constitutional law.

What a very convenient way of clothing official villainy in the garb of constitutional authority! After our corrupt and perjured officials have violated, in a hundred ways, the Constitution they had solemnly sworn to support in order to carry out their nefarious schemes of fraud and plunder, how would it have been possible for them to have contrived a more ingenious device to justify in the eyes of the rising generation their official misdeeds, than by thus adopting, legalizing, and forcing into the public school, through their willing tools, a definition of the word " Constitution " sufficiently elastic to cover every species of their *accustomed* rascalities?

Again! The old Noah Webster of twenty-five years ago, in giving to the word " Union " its political signification, defines it as " STATES UNITED. THUS THE UNITED STATES OF AMERICA ARE SOMETIMES CALLED THE UNION."

But in the false and mutilated Webster which the public-school system now forces our children to study this definition is entirely suppressed, and in its place we have the word " UNION " defined as meaning—

"A CONSOLIDATED BODY, AS THE UNITED STATES OF AMERICA, ARE OFTEN CALLED THE ' UNION.' " Thus, while the real statesmen of both political parties are warning the people against the danger of a consolidated government, the children, who are soon to take the places of these statesmen, through our public-school machinery are indoctrinated with the idea that we already have a consolidated republic. In the case of McCollough *vs.* The State of Maryland, Chief-Justice Marshall, of the Supreme Court of the United States, said: "No political dreamer was ever wild enough to think of breaking down the lines which separate the States and of compounding the American people into a solid mass."

But what no political dreamer was ever wild enough to think of in Judge Marshall's time is now taught as an accomplished fact.

Again, " Webster's Dictionary " twenty-five years ago defined the word " Federal " as—

" CONSISTING IN A COMPACT BETWEEN PARTIES, PARTICULARLY

AND CHIEFLY BETWEEN STATES AND NATIONS FORMED ON ALLI-
ANCE BY CONTRACT OR MUTUAL AGREEMENT, AS A FEDERAL GOV-
ERNMENT, SUCH AS THAT OF THE UNITED STATES." But the
present public-school Webster, after expunging every syllable of
this definition, defines " Federal " as being " specifically composed
of States, and which retain only a subordinate and limited sovereignty, as the Union of the United States and the Sonderbund of
Switzerland."

A moment's reflection will show that under such a definition of
the word " Federal," the several States composing the American
Union would have no rights and no sovereignty which the General
Government would be bound to respect.

Now it is undoubtedly true that in all those matters in which,
under the Constitution, the Federal Government has been clothed
with sovereign authority, the authority of the States is subordinate
to the Federal Government. But in all things else the sovereignty
of the States is as supreme and as independent of the Federal sovereignty as if the Federal sovereignty had never existed.

In the celebrated Dred Scott case the United States Supreme
Court said:

" The principles upon which our Governments rest, and upon
which alone they continue to exist, is the union of States, sovereign
and independent within their own limits, in their internal and
domestic concerns."

But if, as now taught in the public schools of California and elsewhere, the States have no sovereignty except such as is subordinate
to the sovereignty of the United States, what becomes of our sovereign right to local self-government? Suppose that the Federal
Government should to-morrow, in the exercise of its supposed superior sovereignty, undertake to nullify our State Constitution and
laws, abrogate our State Government, remove from office our
Governor, abolish our State Courts and our legislature, and force
us to accept for our local government just such laws as the Federal
Congress might choose to give us, such State, county, and municipal
officers as the President might send to rule over us, what remedy
would we have? Shall I be told that such action on the part of the
Federal Government, clashing, as it would, with the principles of
State sovereignty, would not be tolerated?

But I would answer, if a State possesses no sovereignty except
such as is subordinate to the sovereignty of the Federal Government, would not our subordinate sovereignty be forced to yield to
the superior sovereignty to which it is subordinate? Is it not a law

of nature that whenever two unequal forces meet, the inferior must yield to the superior?

My countrymen, disguise the fact as we may, there is in this country to-day, and in both the political parties, an element which is ripe for a centralized despotism. There are men and corporations of vast wealth, whose iron grasp spans this whole continent, and who find it more difficult and more expensive to corrupt thirty odd State Legislatures than one Federal Congress. It was said of Nero of old that he wished the Roman people had but one head, so that he might cut it off at a single blow. And so it is with those moneyed kings who would rule this country through bribery, fraud, and intimidation.

It is easy to see how, with all the powers of government centered at Washington in one Federal head, they could at a single stroke put an end to American liberty.

But they well understand that before striking this blow the minds of the people must be prepared to receive it. And what surer or safer preparation could possibly be made than is now being made, by indoctrinating the minds of the rising generation with the idea that ours is already a consolidated government; that the States of the Union have no sovereignty which is not subordinate to the will and pleasure of the Federal head, and that our Constitution is the mere creature of custom, and may therefore be legally altered or abolished by custom?

Such are a few of the pernicious and poisonous doctrines which ten millions of American children are to-day drinking in with the very definitions of the words they are compelled to study. And yet the man who dares to utter a word of warning of the approaching danger is stigmatized as an enemy to education and unfit to be mentioned as a candidate for the humblest office.

Be it so. Viewing this great question as I do, not for all the offices in the gift of the American people would I shrink from an open and candid avowal of my sentiments. If I have learned anything from the reading of history, it is that the man who, in violation of great principles, toils for temporary fame, purchases for himself either total oblivion or eternal infamy, while he who temporarily goes down battling for right principles always deserves, and generally secures, the gratitude of succeeding ages, and will carry with him the sustaining solace of a clean conscience, more precious than all 'the offices and honors in the gift of man.

History tells us that Aristides was voted into banishment because he was just. Yet who would not a thousand times rather to-day be Aristides than be numbered amongst the proudest of his persecutors?

Socrates, too, in violation of every principle of justice, was condemned to a dungeon and to death.   Yet what name is more honored in history than his?   And which of his unjust judges would not gladly, hide himself in the utter darkness of oblivion from the withering scorn and contempt of all mankind?

From the noble example of Aristides and of Socrates let American statesmen learn wisdom, and from the undying infamy of their cowardly time-serving persecutors let political demagogues of to-day take warning.

CHAPTER VII.

MISTAKES OF CATHOLICS IN DEALING WITH THE SCHOOL QUESTION.

The New York Catholic Review of November 26th, 1881, published an able article on the educational question, taken from *The Boston Journal of Education*, and in commenting on the same, our Catholic contemporary among other things said :

"*Let it always be borne in mind that we are in favor of free schools, provided they be fair.*"

This, of course, is an entirely safe proposition as stated, because everybody is supposed to be in favor of whatever is *fair*, as he understands the meaning of the word *fair*.   But we are left in doubt as to what kind of free schools our esteemed contemporary would consider *fair*.

Suppose, for example, that all our public schools were such that every child in the land could be educated therein, without any danger either to its health, its life, its morals, or its religion.   In other words, suppose that the public-school system were otherwise perfect, would it be fair to make them free for *all*, and would the editor of the *Review* be in favor of making them *free* for the children of the rich as well as those of the poor?   If he would, then we should like to have him answer one or two other questions, namely : Does not every parent, by virtue of assuming the duties of the parental office, become bound by the natural law to feed and clothe and educate his children?   In other words, is not the education of one's own children a just debt which, if able, he is morally bound to pay?   And if a proper education is a debt which every parent, according to his ability, owes to his own children, upon what principle of fairness or justice can the State take one man's money with which to pay the debt of another?

Again, if feeding, clothing, and educating one's own children are all parental obligations with exactly the same origin, standing upon precisely the same moral footing, and having identically the same binding force, then has not the State the very same right to *feed* and *clothe* that it has to educate, at public expense, the children of parents who are abundantly able to discharge these obligations? And if it is just and fair to raise by general taxation a common fund for the feeding, clothing, and educating of all the children in the country, why is it not equally just and fair to extend the same principle still further, by compelling all to contribute to a common fund for the purpose of feeding and clothing everybody else, as well as everybody's children?

Again, is it fair that the poor old man and his decrepit wife, whom God has never blessed with children, but who have to labor hard sixteen hours a day, the former with his solitary horse and cart, and the latter over her wash-tub, in order to keep soul and body together, should be taxed to help educate the children of the millionaire, who lives in all the splendor of a prince? In other words, would it have been fair to levy upon the rags of Lazarus a tax to pay for educating the children of Dives?

We do not now propose to discuss these questions, but shall await the answers thereto by the learned editor of the *Catholic Review*, and we hope that when we understand each other we shall both be on the same side.

In commenting on the article quoted from the *Boston Journal of Education*, the editor of the *Catholic Review*, while referring to our present public-school system, remarks: "Instead of being a bulwark, it is really a very great danger, as people, *now that Catholics have left off making so much noise about the matter, begin to see for themselves.*"

The intimation which seems to be conveyed by this remark is that agitation of the school question by Catholics necessarily tends to prevent non-Catholics from seeing or acknowledging the evils of the system. That there are some people so blinded by their antipathy to Roman Catholicism that they would not accept any truth upon Catholic authority we do not doubt, but that the great body of non-Catholic Americans are the victims of so blind a bigotry we do not believe, and our convictions are based upon some years of contact with people of all shades of religious and non-religious belief, from the strict followers of Knox and Calvin to the disciples of Thomas

Paine. That there is a very general disposition amongst non-Catholics to distrust the motives of Catholics when agitating this school question is undoubtedly true, but for this distrust we hold that Catholics are themselves very largely responsible. The great evils of the public-school system are such as affect not Catholics alone, but which strike at the authority of every parent, and imperil the welfare, the honor, and the happiness of every family, and consequently any movement against this common foe should from the start have been in the name and on the behalf of the whole people, and not for the benefit of only a small fraction of the people.

When the municipal authorities of New York City, more than forty years ago, were appealed to for relief against the unjust exactions and cruel oppressions of this monstrous system, that appeal, as it seems to us, ought to have been in the name of the people of that city, and for the benefit of the whole people; but instead of that, the petition prepared by, or under the aspices of, the illustrious Archbishop Hughes, which was expected to result in securing their educational rights to a small portion of the inhabitants of that great metropolis, was headed thus:

" *To the Honorable the Board of Aldermen*
             of the City of New York:
    "THE PETITION OF THE CATHOLICS OF NEW YORK RESPECTFULLY REPRESENTS," &c.

The petition then goes on to enumerate the hardships and injustices which Catholics were suffering from this system, seemingly taking it for granted that it was good enough for the rest of mankind.

To this it may be answered that Catholics had some grievances to complain of under the system which non-Catholics had not. This may be very true, but then it is equally true that underlying the whole system was a fundamental wrong which was sapping the foundation of family government, and poisoning the very sources of all domestic happiness, and threatening the downfall and ruin of all civil government and of social order itself. Under these circumstances it was seemingly as illy-advised a movement for Catholics to make an isolated attack upon the system, upon the sole ground of its antagonism to their faith, as it would have been in revolutionary times for the Catholics of old Maryland to have declared war against Great Britain upon the sole ground that she was a Protestant power and imposed unjust burdens upon the Catholics of that colony. Had the Catholics of those days raised such an issue as that, and insisted upon their non-Catholic neighbors aiding them in fighting their battles upon such purely Roman Catholic grounds, instead of planting themselves upon the broad principles of human liberty, which were admittedly as dear to the Virginia Episcopalians and New England Puritans as to themselves, how many recruits outside of their own borders would they have been able to raise for such a war? Here then, we believe, was the first fatal mistake that the Catholics of this country fell into in fighting the school question, namely, the making of it a *Roman Catholic* question instead of a *parental* one. And from that day to this a similar blunder has been periodically perpetrated—only on a smaller scale—in various parts of the country, invariably resulting in widening the breach between Catholics and non-Catholics on this educational question. Another serious blunder—to call it by no harsher name—which many of our Catholics appear to us to have made, is the keeping up of a terrible cry about the Godless public schools, and the injustice of forcing Catholics to pay for their support, whenever they are denied a share in the filthy lucre which pays the price of running the institution; and then subsiding into the utmost docility, and becoming perfectly reconciled to this demon of iniquity the moment they are allowed to pocket the price of the innocent souls which it sends to destruction.

It is evident that one great reason why this class of Catholics—if they can be called such—have made so little impression upon the non-Catholic mind by the " *noise* " they have made about the public-school system was because their course of conduct has not harmonized with their words.

Still another reason is, that there has not been, and is not now, any proper harmony between Catholics themselves. We find priest disagreeing with priest, and layman disagreeing with layman on this vital question. All this appears to us to arise from the fact of ignoring the great and fundamental principles of the natural law which makes it the right and the duty of fathers and mothers, of all creeds and of no creed, to direct and control the education of their own children according to the dictates of their own consciences This is a principle which is dear not only to the Catholic, but to the Protestant, the Jew, and the infidel. It is upon this platform that many of our best and ablest California minds, of all classes of religionists and non-religionists, are beginning to take their stand. And we do but simple justice when we say that, as a general rule, we have found Protestants and other non-Catholics as ready, and oftentimes far more ready, to take their stand with us upon this platform than were many of our co-religionists. If we Catholics would make sure of non-Catholic assistance in our efforts to reform our public-school system, we must first make sure that we, ourselves, are on the right road to such reform, and that our platform of principles is not only right, but broad enough to afford standing room for all child-loving parents, however widely they may differ from us on religious questions. But if Catholics themselves proclaim false principles, they *ought* not to find followers. That some very eminent Catholics have, from time to time, undertaken to maintain very erroneous theories touching this educational question seems to us undeniable. For example, we now have before us a book published in 1876 by the Catholic Publication Society of New York, entitled " *Catholics and Education,*" apparently intended to set forth the position occupied by Catholics on the much vexed school question. The book is made up of articles written by eminent Catholics, and originally published in the *Catholic World.* The following lines from the preface explain the object of this publication :

" The desire to understand the position of Catholics on this subject is wide-spread, and there is a demand among Catholics themselves for more abundant information. These considerations have induced the editor of the *Catholic World* to reprint the following series of articles from the pages of that magazine."

One of these articles, which is thus given to the world as an explanation of " the position of Catholics on this subject," at page 92 contains the following :

" We are decidedly in favor of free public schools for all the children of the land, and we hold that the property of the State should educate the children of the State."

Now for one, we most solemnly protest against the soundness of this so-called Catholic position on the school question. We maintain that it is both Communistic and Pagan. We utterly deny that the State *has* any children. It is true that, by a fiction of the law in use in England, *bastard* children are sometimes called the children of the people. And if the writer of the article from which the above extract is taken intends to say that the property of the State should bear this burden of educating the State's bastard children, we shall urge no particular objection ; but then the question arises, What *is* the property of the State? Surely it is not the property of the private citizen. If the State owns all the property which we have heretofore supposed belonged to individual citizens, the reign of Communism has already begun. If, as seems to be claimed, the State owns all the children and all the property too, we can see no good reason why she may not, and ought not, in common fairness, to make an equal distribution of her own property amongst her own children. After all, this is the true theory upon which rests this Communistic system of public schools.

On page 94, in the course of the same article just quoted, after advocating a general division of the public school money, among such religious denominations as might desire such division, the writer goes on to say : " But we are asked what shall be done with the large body of citizens who are neither Catholic nor Protestant? Such citizens, we reply, have no religion ; and they who have no religion have no conscience that people who have religion are bound to respect. If they refuse to send their children either to Hebrew schools, or the Catholic schools, or, in fine, to the Protestant schools, let them found schools of their own at their own expense."

In other words, let us of the various churches—Catholics, Protestants, and Jews—combine our forces and inflict upon all who *can* not honestly and *will* not hypocritally join some church exactly the same kind of wrong under which we ourselves have been groaning for a long series of years.

If the editor of the *Catholic Review* refers to noises like *these*, we fully concur with him in his intimation that *such* " *noises* " were well calculated to prevent other people from perceiving the evil results of our public schools. But if Catholics will wisely maintain the great principles of human liberty and equal parental rights without regard to differences upon questions concerning either politics or religion, there is no danger but that they will find a ready and cordial response on the part of intelligent and honest people, whether they belong to any church organization or not.

CHAPTER VIII.

THE ROMAN PONTIFFS ON THE PARENTAL RIGHTS OF NON-CATHOLICS—THE EQUAL RIGHTS OF CATHOLICS, PROTESTANTS, JEWS, AND PAGANS UPHELD.

THE following extract from a sermon of Right Rev. Bishop Cameron, delivered at the laying of the corner-stone of a new convent at Sidney, is copied from the Cleveland *Catholic Universe* of November 6th, 1884.

In defining the position of the church on this question of parental rights in educational matters, the learned Bishop says :

" Her principle and practice in this matter were admirably illustrated in the thirteenth century, when the Popes were in the very zenith of their temporal power and influence, and Innocent III ruled the world from the Chair of Peter.   Certain zealots proposed that the infant children of Jews and Mahometans should be forcibly taken away from their parents, baptized and educated as Catholics.   How was the proposal met?   St. Thomas Aquinas, the prince of theologians, repudiated it as a wicked innovation.

" He urged that such was not the usage of the Catholic Church ; that there had been powerful Catholic sovereigns, the Constantines and Theodosii, who had many saintly and enlightened prelates, like Saints Sylvester and Ambrose, to advise them, and that such faithful bishops would not have neglected to recommend the proposed plan, had it been conformable to reason.   He further proved that it was repugnant to natural justice, nature having made the child a thing belonging to the father, the author of its being, and that child, therefore, ought to remain under the parents' care and control until it should attain to the use of reason.   Hence, it would be manifest injustice to withdraw the child in the meantime from the parents, or to do anything to it against the parents' will ; but when the young person has attained the use of his free will, he is then his own, *sui juris*, and is to be led to the church, not by violence, but by persuasion, (212, q. 10, a. 12).   Such was the unanswerable logic with which ' the Angel of the Schools,' the wonder of all ages and the admiration of his own, utterly discredited the proposed encroachment on parental rights, and upheld their inviolable sacredness.

*   *   *   *   *   *   *

" In the best period of Roman society we are told that ' the State presumed not to pass the threshold of the Roman father ' with any educational code in hand, though it did, at a later and worse period, attempt to enforce the tyrannous and novel system imported from captive Greece, which gradually changed and disfigured the fair face of Roman life.   But hostile as was the Roman Empire before its conversion to Christianity, it did not seek to educate the children of Catholics in Paganism, or to prevent Catholic parents from bringing up their children in their own religion.   Even when Julian the Apostate closed the imperial schools to Christian teachers, and forbade Christians to study the Pagan classics and philosophy, he never encouraged the kidnapping of Christian children and the educating of them in the religion of the State.   This is a refinement which exclusively belongs to modern secularism, utterly at variance both with Christian tradition and with the sacredness and inviolability of parental authority.   Representing the temporal order, the State, whether Pagan or Christian, has the right to look after the material wants and interests of society, not after men's minds, ideas, intelligence, motives, and consciences.   The Christian State is bound to use its own powers according to the Christian law, but the Christian law gives it no additional power whatever.   All the power it has is the power belonging to all States, whether Pagan or Mahometan.

A Pagan prince loses no right by his baptism, neither does he gain any new right by it over his subjects. As well, then, might you hold that Nero, Diocletian, or Julian the Apostate, had a right to educate their Christian subjects in the enormities of heathenism, as to maintain that the civil power has now the right to trample on the inalienable right of parents to educate their own offspring as their conscience may dictate. The State, therefore, can interfere in education only as a *helper* of those naturally charged with the education of the young; consequently its first duty, in a community of mixed religions, is that of strict impartiality with regard to the various churches. To employ its educational machinery to protestantize the Catholic, or to catholicize Protestant children, or to *sap* the religious faith of either, would be an intolerable usurpation and injustice. Such a course of proceeding would, instead of helping, *hinder* parents from educating their children according to their conscientious convictions. No; it can never be too often repeated that the State has no right to educate or to control education. For Christian States, as States, are not different from Pagan States, both having the same end and the same matter for their jurisdiction; and who will presume to say that the Pagan State ever had the right to control and direct the education of its Christian subjects? Who will presume to say that it had or has the right to mould Christians' minds, to discipline their understandings, to control their wills, to direct the whole man, and to fashion him after its own prejudices into a so-called good citizen?"

As a most admirable supplement to Right Rev. Bishop Cameron's sermon on parental rights, it affords us great pleasure to be able to present herewith an extract from a letter just received from Right Rev. E. O. Connell, of Marysville, California. The letter was written from Baltimore during the late session of the plenary council, and bears date Nov. 27, 1884. The Right Rev. Bishop says:

" *My Dear Mr. Montgomery:* Some time ago I promised to furnish you with the exact words of the Pope forbidding the least pressure to be put upon *non*-Catholic children attending Catholic schools. But 'tis not till now that I was able to find the precise words, viz:

" ' We forbid non-Catholic pupils attending Catholic schools to be obliged to assist at Mass or other religious exercises. Let them be left to their own discretion.' Instruction of the Sacred Congregation of Propaganda Fide, 25th April, 1868, transmitted to all the Catholic bishops of North America."

These are potent utterances in behalf of liberty, which speak for themselves.

It is our firm belief, founded both on reason and personal experience, that if *all* our American Catholics, bishops, priests, and people, instead of clamoring for special school laws intended for their own exclusive benefit, would boldly and persistently proclaim to the world these broad and universal principles of parental liberty as the inalienable heritage of Catholics, Protestants, Jews, Mahometans, and Free-thinkers, they would soon find their voices heard and their ranks—as the friends of educational reform—swollen by tens of millions of those who are to-day numbered with their bitterest opponents.

CHAPTER IX.

SPECIFICATION OF FATAL ERRORS INHERENT IN THE NEW ENGLAND SCHOOL SYSTEM.

EVERY standard writer on the subject of either law or morals proclaims with one voice that *parents* are bound by the natural law to feed, clothe, and *educate* their own children. Bouvier says : " The " principal obligations which parents owe their children are their " maintenance, their protection, and their education."[1] Chancellor Kent says : " The duties of parents to their children, as being their " natural guardians, consist in maintaining and educating them " during their season of infancy and youth."[2]

Sir William Blackstone says : " The last duty of parents to their " children is that of giving them an *education* suitable to their sta- " tion in life ; a duty pointed out by reason, and of far the greatest " importance of any. For," continues that author, " as Puffendorf " very well observes, ' it is not easy to imagine or allow that a pa- " ' rent has conferred any considerable benefit upon his child by " ' bringing him into the world if he afterwards entirely neglects " ' his culture and education, and suffers him to grow up like a " ' mere beast, to lead a life useless to others and shameful to him- " ' self.' "[3] Dr. Wayland, in his Elements of Moral Science, says : " The duty of parents is generally to educate or to bring up their " children in such manner as *they believe* will be most for their " future happiness, both temporal and eternal."[4] Again : " He " (the parent) is bound to inform himself of the peculiar habits " and reflect upon the probable future situation of his child, and " deliberately to consider *what sort of education* will most con- " duce to his future happiness and usefulness."[5] Again : " The

---

[1] Bouvier's Institutes, vol. 2, p. 118.   [2] 2 Kent, 196.
[3] Cooley's Blackstone, vol. 1, p. 449.
[4] Wayland's Elements of Moral Science, 314.
[5] Wayland's Moral Science, 316.

" duties of a parent are established by God, and God requires us
" not to violate them."[1]   According to the laws of nature, says
Wayland, " the teacher is only the *agent;* the *parent* is the prin-
" cipal."[2]   But, under the New England system, as by law established, the parent is not recognized as the principal, nor is the
teacher regarded as his agent.   The Legislature of California has
gone so far towards elevating the teacher above the parents as to
make it a penal offence for any parent to even insult the teacher
of a public school in the presence of his pupils, no difference what
the provocation may be.

Section 654 of the Penal Code of this State reads : " Every pa-
" rent, guardian, or other person, who upbraids, insults, or abuses
" any teacher of the public schools, in the presence or hearing of a
" pupil thereof, is guilty of a misdemeanor."

If the teacher insults the parent, in the presence of his children,
there is no penalty to pay, or if the dirtiest loafer in the land insults
the teacher of a private school, without the least cause or provocation, *that* is all right; but woe be to the father or mother who has
the temerity to breathe one offensive word against the teacher of a
public school, in the hearing of his pupils, even should it be to chide
him for his immoral conduct towards the child of the offender.

In his biennial report for 1864, our State Superintendent of Public Instruction—quoting from the judicial decisions of some of the
Eastern States, construing their public-school laws, which are in
all respects similar to our own—maintains the proposition that
" *the child should be taught to consider his instructor, in many*
" *respects, superior to the parent in point of authority,*" and
" *that the vulgar impression that parents have a legal right*
" *to dictate to teachers,* is entirely erroneous," and, further, that
" *parents have no remedy as against the teacher.*"[3]   In the State
of Vermont, in 1874, a School Committee expelled from a public
school certain children because of their absence from school on a
religious holiday, although they had remained absent in obedience
to the commands of their parents ; and this, too, was after the school
authorities had been appealed to in vain for leave of absence.   This
action of the School Committee was afterwards sustained by the Supreme Court of the State, which based its decision, in part, at least,
on the ground that " *no Divine authority had been quoted or as-*
" *serted* " to sustain the right claimed by these parents.[4]

[1] Wayland, 321.

[2] Wayland, 316.

[3] See Superintendent Swett's Biennial Report for 1864, pp. 164-5-6, and Judicial Decisions there
quoted.

[4] Ferriter *vs.* Tyler, 48 Vt., 444.

Thus the law of nature and nature's God, which ordains that it is both the right and duty of parents to educate their children " *in such* " *manner as they believe will be most for their future happiness*" is utterly disregarded and set at naught by the State, which ordains that it is neither the right nor the duty of parents, but of the State, to say when, where, by whom, and in what manner our children shall be educated.

Now, it is always possible for either individuals or States to disregard and to violate nature's laws, but it is *not* possible to do so without suffering, sooner or later, a penalty, and a penalty, too, corresponding in magnitude with the importance of the law violated. Hence it is—and we assert it without the fear of successful contradiction—that those communities, which have so long and so glaringly violated nature's laws in the matter of education, are now reaping so heavy and so deadly a harvest of crime, pauperism, insanity, and suicides.

Dr. Wayland has well said " that the relaxation of parental au- " thority has always been found one of the surest indications of the " decline of social order and the unfailing precursor of public tur- " bulence and anarchy."[1] Now, under the law, as we have already seen, parental authority is not merely *relaxed*, but it is utterly set at defiance. What, we would ask, does parental authority amount to, in the matter of educating children, when a parent is not recognized as having any " *remedy, as against the teacher,*" for the wrongs he may perpetrate against his child, and when, as in California to-day, the parent is, in the eye of the law, a criminal who ventures to send his own child to a school of his own choice, and at his own expense, without first going with his hat under his arm to a board of petty officials to beg their *permission* so to do?

If parents, any longer, have the least vestige of authority over the all-important matter of their own children's education, which is not wholly subordinated to the private interests, prejudices, and petty spites of any and every little conclave of irresponsible upstarts who, by hook or by crook, can so manage on election day as to have their names on the tickets of the winning party, we should feel under many obligations if somebody would inform us what that remaining parental authority is, or where it is to be found.

Is it not the almost unanimous cry, on the part of parents, throughout the length and breadth of the land, that they can neither command the respect nor obedience of their children, and are not our

---

[1] Wayland's Elements of Moral Science, p. 313.

police courts crowded, and our county prisons and State penitentiaries being filled with beardless boys, many of whom have had
comfortable homes, and have grown up in the society of respectable
parents, but *never under their control?*

But, perhaps, we shall be asked, why is it that neither politicians
nor the parents of children have thus far done anything towards
furnishing a remedy for all these crying evils?

We answer, the reasons are numerous; but the first and most
important reason we shall assign, is *ignorance:* ignorance of the
true and Heaven-ordained relations between parent and child; ignorance of the reciprocal duties which they respectively owe to each
other; yes, and ignorance—total ignorance—of the foregoing, terrible facts, so clearly revealed by the United States Census Reports.

Let any one who doubts the general ignorance of our people, on
this last subject, test the matter, by catechising the first ten men he
meets concerning the facts shown by our published tables. The
truth is, that the advocates of this New England system have been so
long, so loud, and so persistent in proclaiming to the world its supposed excellencies that nine-tenths of the world have, without the
least investigation, concluded to accept it for all that its most enthusiastic admirers represent it to be. Were it not for the widespread
and almost total ignorance on the part of parents, as regards the
poisonous and deadly fruits which they and their children, and
society at large, are daily reaping from this anti-parental system of
education, it could not survive a single month in its present shape.
O, how true it is that *Ignorance is the mother of vice!*

Another reason why no remedy has been applied to this fearful
malady is a long-standing, deep-seated, and constantly fomented
prejudice in favor of the public-school system, which makes the
politicians afraid to attack the monster lest they hurt their popularity.

STILL ANOTHER DIFFICULTY

is a want of harmony among those who see and 'ament the terrible
evils which this system is bringing on the country, and who are
willing to make any and every sacrifice to avert those evils. One
says, Let us have the Bible in the schools. Another says, No; I want
no Bible in mine. A third says, Let us divide the school funds
amongst all the different religious denominations in such a manner
that each denomination shall, as a body, have control of a portion of
those funds corresponding with the number of its members; while a
fourth says, Away with such silly nonsense; we have far too much
ecclesiasticism in the public schools already. But is there not, we ask,

A COMMON GROUND WHEREON EVERY FRIEND OF EDUCATIONAL REFORM CAN STAND?

Most undoubtedly there is. Let us recognize, just as the law of nature recognizes, the *right* and the *duty* of all parents, having the ability so to do, to educate their own children in their own way and by the use of their own funds.

After all, it is not less the interest than the duty of parents, when they can do so, to pay the cost of their own children's education, and not to allow the State to pay it for them, for be it remembered that the *cost and care of properly feeding, clothing, and educating the child are but the price which Nature demands of parents for the incomparable treasure of the child's love, honor, and obedience, and just in proportion to the extent to which parents neglect or refuse to pay this price, in precisely the same proportion do they forfeit their right to this inestimable boon.*

Let us suppose that the State should take upon itself to feed and clothe, as well as to educate, the child; does any one doubt that a child thus fed, clothed, and educated at the public expense would grow up almost wholly destitute of parental affection? And who is so stupidly blind as not to see that the *education* of the child, after all, is the great nourisher of its affections? Respect, love, and veneration do not depend near so much on either the source or the character of the food which enters the stomach, as upon the source and character of that which is taken into the mind and heart.

But in cases where parents have not sufficient worldly wealth to give their children a good elementary education, let the State aid them just exactly as it should aid them, when necessary, with means to feed and clothe their children, rather than let them either starve or go naked. But for the same reason that the State would not *feed* the children of its more needy citizens upon the most dainty and costly delicacies, nor clothe them in the finest silks and satins, so neither should it *educate* them in those higher or merely ornamental sciences not necessary for those avocations in which they are likely to engage in after life. And when the State furnishes educational aid, let it do so, always, in harmony with the principles of parental guardianship over the child. Let the parent in such cases select the school, and the State pay the teacher. Let this boon be extended to all who need State aid, without regard to differences in politics or religion.

Perhaps, though, we shall be told that so radical a change in the public-school system, as that suggested, would work the destruction of the system itself.   If that be so, then we would ask whether it is better for us to destroy the system, or to let the system destroy us?

Again, it may, perhaps, be objected that even if every parent in the land had the means and the privilege of educating his own children in his own way, still there would always be found some parents in every community who would neglect this most sacred duty ; and what ought to be done with such parents? We answer : What ought to be done with those heartless parents who, having the means at hand, either of their own or such as have been furnished by the State, to comfortably feed and clothe their children, would, nevertheless, deliberately leave them to die of starvation or perish with cold? In either case such parents should be punished as criminals against the laws both of God and society.   But so long as the State undertakes to force upon the children of any class of parents a system of education which they cannot accept without a violation of conscience and of Nature's laws, it is nothing less than the most cruel tyranny on the part of the State to make such a system compulsory.

Let every friend of educational reform unite in maintaining these plain, just, and most reasonable principles, and the day is not distant when—with Heaven's blessing—we shall restore parental authority, re-establish family government, and teach the rising generation to love, honor, and obey, not only their fathers and mothers, but also the laws, both of God and their country.

THE ANTI-PARENTAL SCHOOL SYSTEM DISSECTED AND ANALYZED.

Should we wish to ascertain the exact character and properties of the waters of our great Pacific ocean, we would not undertake to analyze the whole ocean, for that would be an endless task, but we would take up at most a few ounces of this water, and, after making a thorough analysis of it, we would announce the result as indicating the properties and character of the waters of the Pacific.   So it is if we would make a careful and reliable analysis of the essential principles and elements which go to make up what is known as the public-school system.   If we were to undertake to subject to an analytical test the whole system, with its entire paraphernalia of teachers, pupils, parents, school directors, school teachers, school books, school funds, and school houses, as they exist throughout the country, we should become amazed and bewildered at the magnitude of our undertaking, and would probably abandon the enterprise in despair.   So let us take from this very large mass of school material a small quantity of its essential elements, just enough to be handled with ease and examined with care, and we shall be the better able to see what is the character of the ingredients which go to make up the system. In order that you, good reader, may not accuse us of unfairness in our selection of the particular sample to be analyzed, we will allow you to choose your own material. Then cast your eyes around you among your friends and neighbors and name for us two of the very best, purest, most intelligent, highly-educated, and reliable men of your acquaintance. Let them be men of your own religion, and belonging to the same political party as yourself. In a word, let them be two men to whom, in preference to all others in the world, you would be willing to entrust the guardianship of that beautiful little girl of yours, should it please God to take you and and her mother away from her during her years of childhood. Now, these two friends of yours, whom we shall call A and B, we shall take it for granted, are the very best material to be found in that great mass of voters who control by their votes the destinies and shape the character of the public-school system as it exists in your city.

Now, suppose these two mode. men and neighbors should some day come to your house and address you thus : Mr. C., we are informed that you are the father of a bright, beautiful, and intelligent little girl, now about seven years old—just the proper age to begin her education. We feel quite anxious that she should be properly educated, and, to tell you the plain truth, we are afraid that if we leave the matter entirely with you her education will be neglected. Now here is what we propose to do. We propose that we—your two best friends—together with yourself, shall all enter into a written contract, binding ourselves during your daughter's minority to contribute annually a certain percentage upon the assessed value of our property, which shall constitute a fund for the education of this, your little girl. But it must, at the same time, and in the same contract, be stipulated that it shall at all times be in the power of a majority of us three to select the teachers and the school books for your child. Should you, against the wishes and without the consent of a majority of us, take your child away and send her to some other school, you must agree to forfeit—should we choose to exact it—not exceeding twenty dollars for the first offence, and not less than twenty dollars for each subsequent repetition thereof. You must also agree and bind yourself in advance not to withhold your assessment, even should you withdraw your child from the school of our selection, because we should in that event need the money for the education of other children.

Now tell us, good reader, could you ever consent, while living and in the possession of your reasoning faculties, to entrust such a power as this over your infant child—girl or boy—to any two men in existence? Would you not spurn such a proposition as the above with indignant scorn, come from what source it might? We may here remark, in passing, that it surely could not better the matter should these supposed friends and neighbors, in consideration of this proposed outrageous betrayal of your parental trust, even offer to perpetrate a similar wrong against their own children by turning over to you, the insulted father, a corresponding share in their parental authority. And yet, good reader, this miniature picture which we have just drawn of the public-school system presents that system in its very best possible aspect; because we have represented you, the father, as still allowed to retain in your own hands one-third of that parental jurisdiction and control which the God of nature requires you to exercise over your child, while the other two-thirds are to be entrusted to two of the very best men in the whole community. But under the public-school system, as it is by law established, instead of retaining in your own hands even so much as one-third of your parental authority, you retain only an infinitesimal fraction thereof. Where there are, as in San Francisco, tens of thousands of voters, each father divides his parental authority into tens of thousands of equal fragments, retaining but one of these fragments for himself, whilst the great bulk of this authority, instead of being lodged, as in the case above supposed, in two of the very best men to be found in the city, is scattered around broadcast amongst tens of thousands of people, good, bad, and indifferent. It is gobbled up and wielded by every rough and every rake who is allowed to vote; and this is what they call our great American Free-School System.

Those who attempt a justification of this monstrous usurpation of parental authority never fail to intrench themselves behind the hackneyed and much abused maxim, that "the majority has the right to rule." But there are some things in which the majority has no right to rule. For example: The majority has no right to select for a man his religion; neither has it a right to choose for a man the wife, nor for a woman the husband, who is to become a parent of his or her children.

Now the teacher of a child is simply a person who, for the time being, acts as a substitute for its parents. But if a majority has no right to select the *principal*, what right has it to select the *substitute?* In other words, if a majority has no right to force a man or woman, who aspires to become the father or mother of a child, to marry a spouse, to whom he or she objects, on the ground that such a spouse by pernicious teachings or bad example would corrupt the children of such marriage, or poison their minds and hearts against the objecting party, then, in the name of consistency and common sense, what right has this same majority to accomplish the self-same and even worse result, by selecting as the teacher (to take the place of both parents) a person who is distasteful to them and who may imperil and destroy the health, the lives, the honor, the virtue, and the filial affection of their children, as well as their own peace of mind, without in any way being held responsible to them or either of them for his conduct?

CHAPTER X.

A VOICE FROM SAN QUENTIN—CALIFORNIA'S EDUCATED CONVICTS—ALL THE
YOUNGER CRIMINALS CAN READ AND WRITE—TWO MORE PENITENTIARIES
NECESSARY TO ACCOMMODATE MASSACHUSETTS PUBLIC-SCHOOL PUPILS—
CALIFORNIA PUBLIC SCHOOLS THE HIGH ROAD TO THE PENITENTIARY—
HOW THE ONE SERVES AS A PREPARATORY DEPARTMENT FOR THE OTHER.

THE following is from resident director's (Lieutenant Governor Johnston's) biennial report, showing the condition of the California State prison and State prisoners for the two years ending June 30, 1877. This report, under the caption of "Education," says:

"Turnkey's Table, Number VII, showing the educational abilities of the inmates of the prison, gives the number who can read and write at nine hundred and eighty-five ; read but not write, at twenty-four; neither read nor write, at three hundred and nine. If we consider the number of Chinese and Indians in our prisons who can neither read nor write, and deduct them from the whole number so as to match our whites and negroes against the same in other States, it will be found that ours possess the advantage in a large degree. In fact, among the younger convicts they can all read and write."

The Turnkey's Table, Number III, shows that the number of Chinamen in the State prison is 197. Now, if we deduct this 197 from the entire number of convicts who can neither read nor write, it leaves just 112 who can neither read nor write against 985 who can both read and write. Then again, from this 112 there remain still to be deducted the Indians, whose number is not given in the Turnkey's Table. But the most startling revelation contained in the above extract is found in the concluding sentence, which says: "*In fact, among the younger convicts, they can all read and write.*"

Now, of the younger convicts, as appears from the Turnkey's Table, (No. 6,) there are some 253 but twenty-one years old or under, while there are 831 under thirty years old. But while our young State is making such rapid strides in the way of forcing her boys first into her anti-parental schools and then into her penitentiaries, her great exemplar, Massachusetts, it would seem, is not neglectful of her laurels. The regular Boston correspondent of the San Francisco *Morning Call*, under date of November 16, 1877, says: "*The rapid progress of knowledge peculiar to the educational "system of this State has led to the erection of two more State "prisons,* one of which, for women, was successfully opened a "few days ago, the number of wicked females who knocked for "admission being forty-four. Present indications point toward the "rapid filling up of this new institution in a few months."[1]

We are constantly told, by the friends and admirers of our anti-parental educational system, that it is much better and more economical for the State to expend money for schools and school-houses than for jails and penitentiaries. Now, taking the foregoing figures as a basis of calculation, it would be a very interesting process, and would doubtless lead to most important results, if some admirer of our present educational system, who is a good calculator, would make an estimate in dollars and cents of the amount of money saved to the State of California per annum by *that kind* of education, which is sustained at a cost of more than two and a half millions of dollars a year, and which sends to the State prison its hundreds of beardless boys, while total illiteracy—which we all lament as a great evil—sends not so much as one solitary boy to that popular institution.

Should anybody, in making such an estimate, find the profits exceedingly small in proportion to the investment, let him not convert that fact into an argument against education itself, but only against this *anti-parental system* of education; a system which, being conceived in crime, brought forth in crime, and nurtured in crime, must, of necessity, propagate crime. Hoping that some one better versed in figures than ourselves will solve for us the above problem, we shall now proceed to show

HOW IT IS THAT OUR EDUCATED BOYS FIND THEIR WAY TO THE PENITENTIARY.

Here, we will suppose, is an honest, industrious, hard-working laboring man, who has a family consisting of himself, his wife,

---

[1] See *Call* of November 25, 1877.

and half a dozen children, half girls and half boys. To put the case in as favorable an aspect as possible, we will suppose that he is in moderately good circumstances, being out of debt and the owner of a comfortable homestead, but is compelled to rely solely on his own labor and that of his wife for means wherewith to feed and clothe his family. All his children are of an age to attend school, and all are attending the public schools, *as the law directs.* In the first place, heavy and frequent drafts are made on the father's scanty and hard-earned resources in order to supply these children with all the required books and stationery. These six children, too, must each and all be dressed, not according to the means of their parents, but according to the rules of the school and the demands of fashion, and inasmuch as the more wealthy and aristocratic classes prescribe the law of fashion, they must dress as well as the children of the man who counts his wealth by the million. If they do not so dress, they will have to encounter not only the contemptuous sneers of fellow-pupils and class-mates, but, perhaps, the displeasure of teachers, if not expulsion from school. The father would reason and, perhaps, remonstrate with the teacher on the subject of these rigid and extravagant rules of dress, but then he remembers that the law has said that the teacher of a public school is not the agent of the parent, nor answerable to him for his conduct toward the pupil. He also remembers that the law makes it criminal for a parent to insult a teacher, while the teacher may insult the parent with impunity ; and for these reasons he does not care to risk an altercation with the teacher on the subject of the boy's dress ; it would be too unequal a contest. So, in order to meet these growing demands for books, stationery, and clothing for their children, these poor parents are compelled to work harder, dress lighter, and feed more scantily than is compatible with either health or comfort. The father rises earlier in the morning than formerly, works later at night, and goes with worn-out, ragged, or patched-up clothes, in order that his eldest boy may get a new suit so as to make as respectable an appearance as any lad at the Lincoln School.

The mother, too, in worn-out and tattered apparel, plies her washboard with unwonted vigor in order to get money to pay the dressmaker for fitting, cutting, and making Lizzie's nice new dress, for the teacher says she must not come to school looking like an old washerwoman's girl. The daughter, too, is learning to play upon the piano, and of course it will not do for her to lend a helping hand towards washing either clothes or dishes, for the teacher says it will spoil the shape of her fingers and impair the delicacy of her sense of touch. Thus both father and mother work harder than slaves, and dress coarser than beggars, in order that their children may enjoy the great advantages of our glorious free-school system of education.

In the meantime these children are sitting in the same classes, studying the same books, wearing the same costly fabrics, participating in the same amusements, contracting the same habits, imbibing the same love of ease, and the same aversion to manual labor, and the same contempt for manual laborers, as do their far more wealthy and aristocratic school-fellows.

Leaving out of sight the five younger children, we shall now give our undivided attention to the eldest son of this poor laborer.

After years of study he at length completes his course at the Lincoln High School, acquitting himself with great honor, amidst the cordial congratulations of professors and school directors, and eliciting the vociferous applause of the admiring multitude. We may imagine we see his poor old father crouching on the outskirts of the crowd, feasting his eyes upon an occasional glimpse of his boy, but not daring to approach him because he has no clothes fit to be seen on such an occasion; doubtless that father is picturing to himself a brilliant future for his boy. He is, perhaps, looking forward to the time when he shall be a governor, a senator, or possibly President of the United States. Very likely, too, he fancies that in his declining years he shall be able to look to his son for that assistance and support which his own exhausted means may then refuse to afford him. But alas! how baseless are all these castles in the air. The day after quitting school the young man finds himself, for once, thrown on his own unaided resources. His father says to him: "Well, my boy, I have been a long time struggling with poverty and want in order that you might become educated. You see that both your mother and I are in rags, and that handsome suit which you now wear is yet to be paid for. You now have a fortune in your education, and hereafter you must learn to shift for yourself, and, if possible, lend a helping hand from time to time to the support of your younger brothers and sisters."

Thus situated, the young man, probably for the first time in his whole life, asks himself seriously the question: What business he is going to follow. A more appropriate question would be, What business can he follow? There he stands in the midst of a great bustling city, without a cent of money at his command; without friends, without occupation, and without the necessary qualifica-

tions for any earthly employment within his reach.   Probably his
first effort will be to find a position as clerk in some bank or other
business establishment; but he soon learns that these positions are
all filled by the sons of wealthy or influential parents.   Occasionally
he meets a former schoolmate, discharging the duties of some cov-
eted place, but, on inquiry, he learns that he has obtained his position
at the instance of a wealthy father or an influential friend.   Failing
in everything else, he at length seeks for copying as a means of earn-
ing bread.   He gets hold of a city directory and makes a list of the
names and locations of all the law offices in the city.   He then goes
from office to office in quest of the only work he really knows how
to do.   But everywhere he is forestalled ; everywhere he is doomed
to disappointment.   On every hand he meets young men and boys
similarly situated, and making similar fruitless efforts to raise a few
dimes with which to stave off starvation.   Already the boy has spent
weeks in an earnest but vain endeavor to find work as a copyist.   In
the meantime he has been living partly on his old father and partly
on what he could pick up at the free-lunch tables.   Seeing the son's
extreme embarrassment, the father perhaps suggests to him that, inasmuch as he has been disappointed in everything else, he had better come and help him lay down those cobble-stones on Battery street.
where he can at least earn money enough to buy victuals and clothes.
But alas ! his hands are wholly unused to toil, and, what is infinitely
worse, he has been, as we before said, so trained up as to despise both
manual labor and manual laborers.   He would be ashamed for one
of his school companions to even meet him walking the street in company with his own father, because of the old man's horn-like palms
and his laborer's dress ; so that, even if he knew how to work, still,
in view of the fact that it was only the other day that he finished his
educational course with so much *eclat* and amidst such a shower of
bouquets as rained around him from the fair hands of San Francisco's
wealth and beauty, is it to be expected that he is now going to heave
cobble-stones on a public street here, under the very shadow of his
alma mater, to be twitted and jeered at by those who envied him the
literary honors with which he came loaded from the Lincoln school?
No, no ; that is utterly impossible ; propose anything but that.   Yet,
says he, something must be done, and that soon ; I must have clothes,
and I must have bread ; the world owes me a living, and I intend to
have it.   Thus saying, he turns his back upon his humble and destitute home, and betakes himself again to perambulating the streets,
ready for any desperate turn in events that promises him money.

    Let the reader pause here and ask himself the question, What is there to save this youth from becoming a pest to society, a disgrace to his old father and mother, and finally a convicted felon, doomed to serve the State within penitentiary walls? Perhaps it will be claimed that the bare recollection of his newly acquired literary honors, and the fear of losing the esteem of those who, the other day, so vociferously applauded his youthful oratory and threw at his feet such a profusion of flowers, ought, of itself, to be sufficient to shield him from temptation's harm. But, unfortunately, those withered flowers will not serve for food, nor can he make clothes either of approving smiles or shouts of applause. But can it be possible, you say, that one so young, so intelligent, and so well educated has no respect for the law? Why, sir, if you talk to him about respecting the law he will laugh you to scorn. Who is it that respects the law, he will say, except just so far as the law subserves his purposes? Have we not laws against bribery? And yet do not even our law-makers, on election days, send out their dirty minions with money in their pockets with which to buy their way into the very halls of legislation? Are not seats in the United States Senate sometimes bought with gold? And does not even the election of a United States President often depend more upon successful lying, frauds, and bribery, than upon the people's honest votes? Then why prate to me about the sanctity of the law when the very men who make the laws trample them unceremoniously under their feet whenever it suits their purposes? But, you will say, if this youth has no regard for human law, surely he cannot be wholly indifferent to the laws of God. Be not so fast, my dear sir. Have you forgotten that the boy was educated in our public schools, where it is a criminal offence, punishable by a forfeiture of all interest in the public school moneys, to even mention the subject of religion in the hearing of a pupil? And do you know that there is no such prohibition against inculcating the horrible doctrines of atheism in these schools? That many of our public-school teachers are avowed atheists, who believe neither in God nor devil; neither in hell nor heaven; and that our young hero is a firm believer in these dismal and diabolical doctrines? Very true, you say; I knew very well that no religion was allowed to be taught in the public schools, but then why did not his father and mother teach him religion at home?

We first answer the question by asking another, and it is this: How do you know that his parents themselves had any well defined notions of religion, or, in fact, any religion at all? If they had firmly believed in the teachings even of that natural religion which an Almighty hand has written in indelible characters on every human heart, they surely would never have consented to surrender to the public at large the right to select the teachers, and in all essential particulars to shape the mental and moral as well as the physical destinies of their child.

But suppose that his parents were in every other particular real models of perfection, both in their professions and in their practices of religion, was it to be expected that he, their son, would accept religious instruction from them? Are not they illiterate, and is not he educated? And shall wisdom take lessons from ignorance? Has he not learned to despise them both for their poverty and their simplicity? Can it be doubted that even the sacrifices which they made in his behalf; that the very patches with which they mended their old garments, in order that he might be handsomely dressed; that the very toils and hardships which have wrinkled their brows, soiled their features, and imparted the bony touch to their palms, in order that he might learn to lead a life of ease and freedom from manual labor, are, on his part, requited with coldness and contempt? And after learning to despise his parents, is it at all likely that he would profit either by their religious instruction or their praiseworthy example? No, no; their religion, just like their toilsome lives and their old clothes, may be good enough for them, but to an educated young man like himself it is only a bundle of cumbersome and useless rubbish, and he will have none of it.

Then, since our young hero has learned to respect neither the laws of man nor the laws of God, and will neither be directed by the good counsels nor influenced by the exemplary lives of his own father and mother, where, let it be asked, shall we look for the controlling power that is to shape his future destinies? Just follow him as he hurries along yonder busy street and you shall see. Already he is in company with half-a-dozen of his late school-mates, each of whom has a tale of woe and disappointments to tell, quite like his own. Now, for the first time since leaving school, each and all of these boys find themselves in congenial society. They feel that the world cares nothing for them, and they care nothing for the world. They all have empty stomachs and seedy clothes, and there is not money enough in the crowd to purchase even one night's lodging at the meanest lodging-house in the city.

One of the party suggests that, having failed in everything else, he has an idea of making an effort to get a position as dish-washer in some hotel, or, failing in that also, he might seek employment as stable-boy to clean out the stalls of some livery stable. The majority of his companions, however, frown down the proposition with contemptuous indignation, and our hero threatens never hereafter to speak to the low-bred rascal should he ever again be guilty of advancing a proposition so far beneath the dignity of an educated gentleman. In order, however, to put at rest the question as to the feasibility of finding even that kind of employment, one little fellow, the smallest in the crowd, puts in a word to assure his companions that there is not enough in the last suggestion to be worth quarrelling about. He says he has been, for the past three days and a good part of the nights, hunting from house to house, both in public hotels and private dwellings, for any kind of light work such as boys could do, and everywhere he has found the field already occupied, most always by Chinamen; whereupon they all agree that they could not if they would, and would not if they could, enter into successful competition with Chinamen for the honor of discharging the menial duties of either stable boys or kitchen servants.

At this particular juncture one of the party suggests that his old widowed aunt has $500 in gold twenties buried under her barn floor, and that he knows just where to find the cash. They can get this money and nobody but themselves need be any the wiser for it. He says she has plenty without that, and she is such a stingy old hag that it would be serving her just right for them to go and relieve her of that five hundred. We do not propose to follow this little band of young hoodlums farther for the present, but if any friend of our present public-school system can discover any motive which will deter from crime and preserve from the penitentiary any one of the hundreds upon hundreds of our city's youths, whose education and situation in life differ in no essential particular from that of the boys just above described, he will by pointing out such a motive unquestionably confer a great and lasting benefit both on the rising generation and on society at large. From the fate of this eldest boy of our poor laborer we shall leave the reader to guess the doom which awaits his younger brothers and sisters.

CHAPTER XI.

THE POLITICAL STATE AS A TEACHER OF MORALITY.

SECTION 1702 of our California School Law provides, among other things, that " *It shall be the duty of all teachers to endeavor* " *to impress upon the minds of the pupils the principles of mo-* " *rality.*"

But just here the question arises, " What is morality ?" And how is a teacher to know what it is that he or she is required to teach in order to comply with this requirement of the statute?

The immortal Washington has said : "*Let us with caution indulge the supposition that morality can be maintained without relig- ion.*" But if morality cannot be maintained without religion, then how is it possible, we would inquire, for the teacher to inculcate the principles of morality without inculcating the principles of religion ? But the principles of religion are understood by the Jews differently from what they are by the Christians, and by the Roman Catholics differently from what they are by Protestants, by the Episcopalians differently from what they are by the Presbyterians, by the Presby- terians differently from what they are by the Unitarians, and by those who reject the authority both of the Old and New Testament differ- ently from what they are by either Jews or Christians of any denom- ination whatever.

Then how is it possible for the State to require the teaching of morals in the public schools without requiring as the basis of such teaching the inculcation of religious principles, such as are necessa- rily antagonistic to the conscientious convictions of the parents of at least a portion of the children attending these schools ? It is true we hear a great deal about the " *broad principles of common mo- rality* " and of a common religion, but we have never yet had the good fortune to find anybody who was able to give a definition of this common morality or common religion to the perfect satisfaction of any one, except perhaps it was the self-conceited author of such definition.

A certain professor of our State Normal School, to whom we not long ago addressed an open letter, (which, by the way, we believe has never been answered,) in an address of his which was published in the May number of the *Defender*, 1881, took the ground that " the ethics of the Ten Commandments and of the Sermon on the Mount are as absolutely unsectarian as the law of gravitation." Now to assume that the Commandments and the Sermon on the Mount are absolutely unsectarian is to assume that people of all religious sects or denominations, as well as all non-religionists, understand them in the same sense, and accept them as coming with the same author- ity and having the same binding force.

But is it true that people of all religious denominations, as well as non-religionists, do understand either the Ten Commandments or the Sermon on the Mount in the same sense ; or as coming with the same authority, or as having the same binding force? We say no !

Most emphatically no. Waiving the differences in the various translations of these important parts of the Bible, we shall proceed at once to consider some of the various and conflicting beliefs which have been made to rest for their foundation either upon those Ten Commandments or upon the Sermon on the Mount. Take, for example, the commandment, "Remember thou keep holy the Sabbath day," and we find even Christians differing widely as to whether under the Christian dispensation the keeping holy of the Sunday is a sufficient compliance with the requirements of that commandment. As an illustration of this fact we may remark that the leading printing and publishing house of Oakland, and in fact one of the foremost establishments of its kind on the Pacific coast, is owned and run by an association of Christians who would conscientiously regard it as a sin to do unnecessary work on a Saturday; and we all know that pretty much our entire Jewish population entertain a similar belief. But not only do our people differ as to the particular day which is required by the above commandment to be kept holy, but they differ also as to the proper mode of keeping it holy. Thus, the Catholic believes that unless released from the obligation by some lawful excuse, such as distance, sickness, or the like, he should sanctify the Sunday, in part at least, by assisting at mass, while other Christian denominations recognize no such obligation. Some Christians believe it sinful to engage in hunting, fishing, or almost any kind of amusement on the Sunday, while others, equally conscientious, regard these pastimes as harmless. Then, again, a large number of people disbelieve both in the Old and New Testament, and consequently do not look upon the commandment to keep holy the Sabbath day as having any binding force. We here state these different views with reference to the above-quoted commandment, not for the purpose of discussing the question as to which are right and which are wrong, but for the purpose of showing that such differences exist; and in view of the fact that they do exist, we maintain that it is impossible for the public-school teacher to teach said commandment according to any of said views without violating Section 1672 of our public-school law, which declares that "no sectarian or denominational doctrine must be taught therein." Perhaps we shall be told that the commandments should be taught just in the words in which we find them, without interpretation or comment. But let us see for a moment how this would work. Here is a ten-year-old boy, we will suppose, who has just read from his Bible the command, "Remember thou keep holy the Sabbath day." The boy being naturally of an inquiring mind, turns to his teacher and asks the very natural question, " What is the Sabbath day?" What ought the teacher under such circumstances to say? Ought he to say, I don't know; or, I am not allowed to tell you, because to tell you would be sectarian teaching? To such an answer, the boy in his own mind would probably reply, " Of what earthly use is this command to keep holy the Sabbath day, if I am not to know what the Sabbath day is?" And suppose that the boy, still pressing his inquiry, asks the further question, " In what way am I to keep the Sabbath holy? What is it necessary to do, and what necessary to abstain from doing in order to obey this commandment?" Must the teacher again reply, " I am not allowed to tell you."

If anything in the world is calculated to bring both the teacher and the Bible into ridicule, we think that such a teaching as this would surely accomplish that result.

We do not propose in this connection to discuss the question as to the State's right to enact and enforce Sunday laws; but we may remark in passing that it appears to us as if legislation in that direction ought to be limited to the enactment of such laws as have for their object the protection of citizens in the uninterrupted discharge of what they believe to be their religious duties, and not such as may be designed to compel an observance of the Sunday in any particular manner for the spiritual welfare of those thus compelled. We think there would be but little merit in a man's attending church on a Sunday, not for the love of God, but for the love of the *money* which he might have to pay as a fine for his failure to attend. Persecutions against conscience may make hypocrites, but never genuine converts to the doctrines thus sought to be enforced.

With reference to the Sermon on the Mount, its different interpretations are no more harmonious than are those of the commandment referred to. Even people professing themselves Christians differ widely as to whether that sermon was a divine or only a human utterance. The Unitarians, for example, not believing in the divinity of Christ, only look upon that sermon as a human production, while other Christian denominations accept its every word as the infallible teaching of infinite wisdom; so that the teacher cannot undertake to tell his pupil in the public school, after reading to him that sermon, whether he is to accept it as the word of God or only as the word of a man, without again invading the realms of denominational teaching. And all will admit that there is an infinite difference between the weight to be attached to the language of an All-wise God and even the wisest utterances of a mere man when giving expression to the deductions of his own finite and feeble reason. Then, again, as it is with the interpretation of the commandments so it is with the interpretation of the Sermon on the Mount. There are many passages in that sermon which are very differently construed by people of different religious denominations. For example, it is there said, " Ye have heard that it was said to them of old, Thou shalt not forswear thyself, but shall perform unto the Lord thine oaths ; but I say unto you, Swear not at all." This passage is by many very conscientious people interpreted as prohibiting the taking of an oath as a witness or otherwise, and hence they never swear, even in our courts of justice, but affirm.

Again, it is said in the Sermon on the Mount, as read in the Douay Bible, " If thy right eye scandalize thee, (or as the new version has it, ' *cause thee to stumble*,') pluck it out and cast it from thee, for it is expedient for thee that one of thy members should perish, rather than that thy whole body go into hell." Now suppose that some public-school teacher, when reading or having read this passage to his pupils, should be asked the question, "What is the meaning of hell ? " what answer could he give which would not be sectarian or denominational in its character ? How could he so frame a definition of the word "hell" as to make it acceptable both to the Universalist and the Presbyterian, or the Roman Catholic ?

In this same sermon it is said : " When thou fastest, anoint thy head and wash thy face that thou appear not to men to fast, but to thy Father, who is in secret, and thy Father who seeth in secret will repay thee." Now, if the public-school teacher were asked by a pupil whether this passage was to be taken as a Divine authority for the practice of fasting, how could he answer this question without again violating that section of the Code which forbids all sectarian or denominational teachings in the public schools ?

Again, Christians of some denominations interpret the Sermon on the Mount as authorizing the absolute dissolution, by divorce, of the valid bonds of matrimony for certain causes, so as to allow one of the divorced parties to marry again during the life of the other, while other Christians maintain that all such second marriages during the lives of both the divorced parties are, morally speaking, invalid and wrong.

Indeed, it would require a volume to point out all the different interpretations which have been placed upon the Ten Commandments and the Sermon on the Mount. How, then, is it possible to teach even these portions of the Bible in the public schools without teaching sectarian or denominational doctrine ? It certainly would not be called *teaching* in any *other* educational institution in the

wide world (except it be an American public school) to simply
cause the pupil to pronounce, like a trained parrot, a certain form
of words and at the same time refuse to tell him the meaning of
those words.

Our conclusions, then, are these, namely: First; that Washington was right, when he said: " Let us with caution indulge the
supposition that morality can be maintained without religion."
Second; that the State cannot teach morality without teaching
religion as its foundation. Third; that the State cannot teach either
morality or religion without either establishing a new religious
denomination, or else teaching it as it is taught by some one of the
existing denominations. Fourth; that the State can neither teach
religion as it is now taught by any existing denomination, nor as it
might be taught by a State-begotten denomination, without a fatal
infringement upon the doctrine of religious liberty; and that, therefore, the true and proper business of the State is not to teach nor
to pay for teaching either morality or religion, but to foster and
encourage the teaching of both, by carefully and scrupulously
guarding and protecting the equal rights of all citizens to worship
God and to educate their children according to the dictates of their
own consciences.

We say, let the State neither undertake to teach nor to pay for
the teaching of morality or religion, because it is impossible to teach
a State morality without teaching a State religion, and it is impossible to teach a State religion without the destruction of the religious
liberty of the citizen. Should the State ever assume the burden
of paying for religious teaching, its next step would logically be to
assume the right to say what that religious teaching should be. It
is in order to make it harmonize with the principles here asserted
that the seventh proposition of our platform is so framed as to
allow every parent, whose child is entitled to receive a secular education at public expense, to select the school wherein that secular
education shall be given, so that if in obedience to conscience he
elect so to do, the parent may without cost to the State secure for
such child a moral and religious training at the same time that, at
the State's expense, it is receiving its secular training.

In order to do this, we see no practical way, except to pay the
teacher, not according to the *time* he is employed in teaching, but
according to his success in imparting to his pupils secular knowledge—the only kind of knowledge for which (as we believe) the
State can venture to pay without ultimate danger to the principles
of religious liberty We can see no more objection to the State's

paying a religious teacher according to results for imparting secular knowledge to a child which has to be educated at public expense than there would be in its paying a religious stone-cutter by the job for dressing a certain quantity of building stone to be used in the erection of a public building.

If two stone-cutters are working by the piece for the Government, and one of them works and curses, while the other works and prays, we can see no good reason why the man who prays should get less pay for his work than does the man who curses, for work of precisely the same quality and quantity. So, likewise, if there be two teachers working by the job for the Government in the business of teaching children to read, write, and cipher, and if one of them should teach Tom Paine's "Age of Reason" as a reading book, scoff at everything which Christians regard as sacred, and finally complete his work by turning over to the State a score of infidel scholars, perfect in reading, writing, and arithmetic, while the other uses the Bible as a class-reader, speaks reverently of God and religion, and eventually graduates from his school some twenty Christian gentlemen, perfect masters of the three R's, would there be any good reason why the first-named teacher should be paid for his secular teaching and the other get nothing for his?

In the cases supposed we would ask the State to pay nothing for inculcating the principles of Tom Paine, and nothing for teaching the doctrines of the Bible, but in each case we would have the teacher paid for teaching his pupils how to read without regard to the fact that in one case they had used Paine's "Age of Reason," and in the other case the Bible as a class-book. And we would do this, not because we claim that there is any comparison between the writings of Tom Paine and the Bible, but because we are opposed to having the State step between the parent and the child in a matter of so much importance as that which concerns the child's education touching religious subjects.

If we recognize the State in its political capacity as having the right to decide for us and for our children as to the relative merits of the Bible and Tom Paine's "Age of Reason" as class-books, we virtually agree to stand by its decision ; and for a Christian to agree to stand by its decision would, in effect, be to agree to apostatize from his faith whenever the State demands such a sacrifice.

To reiterate our position, the principle for which we are contending is not that the political State ought to enforce the teaching of some particular kind of religion, or any religion at all, but that it ought to leave parents perfectly free to obey the dictates of their own consciences in that regard.

It has sometimes been suggested that the plan we propose might enable the teacher to proselytize his pupils to his own faith against the will and consciences of their parents. To this suggestion we reply that one of the very strongest arguments in favor of this plan is that it would place in the hands of the parents of each child the very best possible safeguard against such proselytizing. The safeguard to which we allude is found in the fact that, upon the very first intimation of any such proselytizing, the parent could and would withdraw his child from school and thereby diminish the teacher's pay. In that regard the proposed system would be infinitely superior to the present one; for it is a well-known fact that, notwithstanding the statutory law forbidding the teaching of sectarian doctrines in the public schools, yet whenever the teachers, the school directors, and a majority of the public in any given locality have a leaning in favor of or against any given sect, that fact is pretty sure to make itself felt in the public-school room, either in the books used or the instruction given. Under such circumstances, the teacher has everything to gain and nothing to lose by overriding the law and the rights of those belonging to the unpopular creed, in obedience to the wishes of the more popular sect, at whose will and pleasure he holds his position and draws his salary. Under the plan which we propose, the teacher or principal of each school, being master of his own time and the author and architect of his own discipline, could easily adjust matters in such a way as to give moral and religious instructions to the children of such parents as might so desire without any encroachment upon either the time or the religious prerogatives of pupils belonging to a different faith or to no faith at all. In proof of this we need but to look around us right here in the cities of Oakland and San Francisco, where there are scores and scores of private schools being taught, in some instances by Presbyterians, in others by Congregationalists, in others by Methodists, in others by Roman Catholics, etc., and in pretty nearly, if not quite, all of these schools there are pupils whose parents belong some to one creed and some to another, and some to no creed whatever, and there are classes in which denominational doctrines are taught to those children whose parents desire it without the least interference with others whose parents are of a different way of thinking.

We frequently hear of troubles and contentions in the public schools, though pretendedly non-sectarian, because of the sectarian teachings therein practised, in defiance both of the statutory law and of the rights of parents and children, while in schools professedly denominational we seldom or never hear of any such complaint.

The reason of this difference is obvious. In the former case the teacher is not amenable to the parents of his pupils, but in the latter he is.

We want no Board of Education, sitting in judgment, to determine whether certain teachings in the public schools are antagonistic to the faith of some of the parents whose children attend these schools. If parents themselves do not know what they religiously believe, we are at a loss to know how a board of politicians, called school directors, can inform them. We want no State standard for either morality or religion. If any one desires to see a specimen of State morals and State religion as taught by State authority, let him read the recent proceedings of the California State prison investigating committee. In the course of those proceedings the fact was revealed that certain convicts, whose terms of penal service for crimes of which they stood convicted were about expiring, and against whom other criminal charges were awaiting trial in the courts, found in their moral instructor a most willing and efficient adviser and assistant in their efforts to baffle the officers of the law, avoid re-arrest, and thus defeat the ends of justice. Such is *State* morality, taught under *State* authority, and at the *State's* expense.

CHAPTER XII.

THE AUTHOR INTERVIEWED ON THE SCHOOL QUESTION.

THE following is from *The Oakland* (California) *Mirror* for December, 1881 :

Last week Mr. Montgomery returned to Oakland from San Diego, where he has recently purchased a ranch, and was soon called upon by our reporter on educational matters, who informed him that Gen. Eaton, United States Commissioner of Education, had recently been in Oakland and stated he had heard in Washington of an anti-public-school man in California named Zach. Montgomery, and that he should like to know more of him and his peculiar views, and that he had exacted a promise from him (the reporter) to interview this odd Californian, and to send him a copy of such interview.

" Sit down," said Mr. Montgomery.

The reporter returned thanks and seated himself, with pencil and note-book in hand, and, after learning incidentally that his hospitable host was a native of Nelson county, Kentucky, the interview then opened vigorously and ran as follows:

REPORTER. Now, Mr. Montgomery, have you any objections to answering a few questions relative to your object in withdrawing from the legal profession and devoting yourself to the agitation of the school question and the progress which that agitation is making?

Mr. MONTGOMERY. None in the world, sir. This agitation concerns the public, and the public have a right to know all about it.

REPORTER. Is it true that your object is to procure a division of the public-school funds upon what is called a sectarian basis, upon a plan similar to that once proposed by Archbishop Hughes, of New York?

Mr. MONTGOMERY. No, sir, it is not true; and I will further state that, while I am a firm believer in the doctrines and teachings of my own church, the Catholic, I now am, and always have been, utterly opposed upon principle to the State's taxing any class of citizens to pay for teaching anybody's children any kind of doctrines or principles touching the subject of religion, either *pro* or *con*, when the citizens thus taxed or any of them do not believe in the doctrine so taught.

REPORTER. Will you be good enough, for the benefit of the readers of *The Mirror*, to give me a brief outline of your true position on this educational question?

Mr. MONTGOMERY. Certainly, sir, since you desire it. My views in brief I keep as standing matter on the last page of my *Review*, the *Family's Defender*, epitomized in the shape of seven short propositions, which are substantially as follows:

I maintain, in the first place, that the cost of educating children, just like the cost of feeding and clothing them, is a debt which every parent owes to his own children, and that it is as unjust to take one man's money with which to educate the children of another who is able to educate them himself as it would be to take one man's money to buy victuals and clothes for children whose parents have the means wherewith to feed and clothe them. Hence, I contend that education, at public expense, ought to be limited to those children whose parents are unable to educate them. I further contend that, as a rule, education, when at public expense, should be restricted to the elementary English branches, coupled with such an industrial education as will fit the party educated to earn an honest living. I believe, also, that the whole business of teaching school should be thrown open to private enterprise and free competition, just like practising law or medicine or running a shoe factory; and then I would allow every parent who is deemed fit to be the guardian of his own children to select the particular school wherein they are to be educated. I would have as our only school officers one or more examiners, either elected or appointed for each district, whose duty it should be to periodically examine, in the legally appointed secular branches, all such pupils as are being taught at public expense, and to report upon the value of the teacher's services as indicated by the progress of his pupils, so that he might be paid according to that value.   I would have no questions asked as to whether the teachers were Catholics, Protestants, Jews, or Free-thinkers; or whether, in addition to the secular training given at public expense, these same teachers had, either gratuitously or at private expense, and at the request of parents, given religious instructions to any or all of their pupils.

REPORTER. By limiting education at public expense to the common English branches, would not many of our brightest youths be deprived of the possibility of obtaining such an education as is at all in keeping with their talents, and the State thereby be made the loser?

Mr. MONTGOMERY. I said, " *as a rule*," education, when at public expense, should be thus limited, but most general rules, you know, have their exceptions; and, in this case, I would make an exception in favor of such youths as possess extraordinary talent for any particular science, coupled with a corresponding degree of merit.

REPORTER. But where and how could you draw the line between those parents who are and who are not able to educate their children at their own expense?

Mr. MONTGOMERY. There may be many ways of drawing this line, but in the absence of a better way I would suggest that the law be so framed as to require every parent who has children of school age, and who is worth a given sum per child to be educated, over and above his debts and liabilities, exclusive of property exempt from execution, to educate his own children at his own expense, and to allow all parents, worth less than the designated sum, to have their children educated at the public's expense.   In this way the assessor's returns could be made to settle the question as to who are and who are not able to educate their own children.

REPORTER. Suppose this plan were to be adopted, what disposition could be made of all our public-school property?

Mr. MONTGOMERY. Why, sir, without doubt it would all be in immediate demand for educational purposes.   You must remember that the same children who are now attending school would still have to be educated.   It is true there would not be nearly as many of them studying the so-called higher branches, but what would be far better, thousands of children would be perfecting themselves in spelling, reading, writing, and arithmetic, who are now neglecting these essential branches in order to get a mere smattering in drawing, music, or the foreign languages.

REPORTER. You will excuse me, Mr. Montgomery, but I do not yet see how, under your proposed plan, all our public-school grounds, houses, and furniture could be made available.   All these are public property, while your plan would virtually turn over the great body of our children to private schools, and this, it seems to me, would necessarily leave our public-school property vacant.

Mr. MONTGOMERY. I was just going on to explain that, under the plan suggested, private schools would be vastly multiplied and, in order to carry on these private schools, school-grounds, houses, and furniture would be absolutely necessary, so that the public-school property could be easily rented or sold to private-school educators. And inasmuch as the most competent and successful educators would get the most patronage, *they* are the persons who could afford to pay the highest prices for this public-school property ; and, therefore, they are the ones who in future would educate our children.

REPORTER. And what disposition would you make of the funds arising from the rent or sale of our school property?

Mr. MONTGOMERY. I would have the rent of all this property, or the interest on the money arising from the sale of it, used to pay for educating in the proper English branches all such children as could not otherwise get such education.   There are now upwards of $6,000,000 worth of public-school property belonging to this State, and there is scarcely a doubt but that the rent of this property, or the interest upon its value, would be nearly, if not quite, sufficient to give to every child in this State, whose parents are not able to educate it, a far better education than can now be obtained, under the present system, by the annual expenditure of $3,000,000, in addition to the use of this $6,000,000 worth of school property.

REPORTER. If I understand you, then, your opinion is that the adoption of the proposed plan would save to the people of this State at least $3,000,000 per annum in the single item of school taxes, and at the same time vastly improve the educational advantages of the rising generation?

Mr. MONTGOMERY. Yes, sir, that is exactly my position.

REPORTER. Do you find many persons who agree with you in these views?

Mr. MONTGOMERY. Why, sir, the fact is I seldom find a man who dissents from them, when he understands them.   As an evidence of the intrinsic popularity of these views witness the overwhelming endorsement they received after full discussion, in the old Congregational church in Oakland, at a large meeting presided over by the State Superintendent of Public Instruction, who, as is well known, used his utmost endeavors, even as a presiding officer, to defeat their adoption.   Witness also the fact that almost every leading clergyman, both of Oakland and San Francisco, including upwards of twenty Protestant ministers and a number of Jewish rabbis, besides many of the prominent officers of every shade of politics, as well as lawyers, doctors, and thinking men in all the various walks of life, have signed a petition asking that these same views be submitted to a vote of the people as a preliminary step towards so changing our State Constitution as to make it harmonize with them.

REPORTER. If it is not too much of a digression, I should like to know what you think of the fear that is sometimes expressed on account of the growth of Roman Catholicism in this country, and its supposed antagonism to the principles of liberty?

Mr. MONTGOMERY. Well, sir, I will tell you candidly what I think about that.   Should the Government of this country ever fall into the hands of *such* Catholics as endorse the present public-school system other denominations may well tremble for their liberty, as you can readily see. This system, as you know, rests upon the assumption that a majority of the people have a right to determine whether any, and, if any, what kind of religion shall be taught in the public schools, and to compel the minority to submit to that determination. Now let us suppose that this majority should be composed of a class of so-called Catholics, who *believe* in this monstrous doctrine that in educational matters the minority has no rights which the majority is bound to respect, will you tell me what is to prevent a majority composed of *such* Catholics as these from forcing the children of a helpless minority of Protestants to study the Catholic catechism in the public schools, provided that by so doing they can make themselves popular and put money in their pockets?

REPORTER. Of course they could not do that without violating our present constitution.

Mr. MONTGOMERY. Very true; but written constitutions you must remember furnish only feeble barriers against unwilling majorities, and that for two reasons, namely, such majorities can either change the existing constitution or override it with impunity.

REPORTER. Do you really think that the Catholics of whom you speak, even if they had the power, would ever so use that power as to oppress their Protestant neighbors?

Mr. MONTGOMERY. Well, sir, *you* might trust them, but I could not; and I will tell you why. These same Catholics—if I may call them such—are now helping to use exactly this same power for the cruel and unjust oppression of other Catholics, as well as non-Catholics, who do not believe as they do in the immaculate character of the present public-school system, and I can scarcely think that they would deal any more liberally or more justly with Protestants, Jews, or Free-thinkers than they are now dealing with their co-religionists, especially when by so doing they would sacrifice both their popularity and their self interest. It is true that they can find no warrant in the authoritative teachings of their church for forcing upon non-Catholic children religious teachings which are repugnant to the consciences of their parents; but neither can they find there any warrant for forcing upon the children of either Catholics or non-Catholics, in defiance of the protesting consciences of their fathers and mothers, the Godless, vicious, and crime-breeding system of education which now curses our land from the shores of the Atlantic to the shores of the Pacific.

CHAPTER XIII.

THE GREAT BATTLE GROUND ON WHICH THE EDUCATIONAL QUESTION MUST BE FOUGHT.

IT must be clear to every thinking mind that the chief reason why the present anti-parental and crime-producing public-school system has obtained so strong a hold upon the country is to be

found in a want of united and harmonious action on the part of
those who see and lament its pernicious influence over the rising
generation, but differ as to the precise thing which constitutes the
fundamental evil of the system, and consequently they equally
differ as to what ought to be the remedy for said evil.   For
example : Many honest and conscientious people believe that the
great wrong committed by the political State, through its public-
school system, consists in its prohibiting the reading of the Bible
in the public schools, while many others, equally conscientious
and equally opposed to the present system, believe that the State
is right in forbidding the use of the Bible in the schools, but that
it is wrong in allowing " Johnson's Cyclopedia " and certain other
books, believed to have either a sectarian or a partisan bias, to be
taught in these schools.   Still another class object to the system,
because of the immoral or incompetent character of many of its
teachers, or because of the objectionable methods of teaching in
use in its schools, or because of the commingling of the sexes, or
for other kindred reasons.

But to our mind, the chief vice of the system lies in its usurpation of parental authority, and in its attempting to do for each
child, through political agencies, that which can be properly done
by nobody else in the world, except by its own father and mother.
We contend that this usurpation of parental authority by the political State is the main trunk out of which naturally grow the other
evils just mentioned, and that, until this parent tree be rooted up,
we shall never be able to rid our country of its poisonous branches,
or their bitter and deadly fruits.

The question which we are discussing, and the question which
we urge every intelligent citizen to consider, is not whether the
Bible ought or ought not to be read in school ; nor whether
" Johnson's Cyclopedia " is a proper book for school libraries ;
nor whether a particular class of teachers are or are not the best
adapted to school work ; nor whether the commingling of the sexes
in the schools has a moralizing or a demoralizing tendency ; nor
whether the teaching of religion and the physical sciences ought or
ought not to go hand in hand ; nor whether good children, who
have been carefully and morally trained at home, ought or ought
not to be sent to the same school with the vicious and depraved,
with the view of reforming the latter.   That there is a wide and an
honest difference of opinion amongst the American people as to
these questions no candid and intelligent citizen will deny.   And
accepting this honest difference of opinion as an existing *fact*, the

question which we now propose to discuss is this: Does it rightfully belong to the political State to determine these questions for
parents and children, and to compel them to submit to its decision?
If the political State has the right to decide these questions for parents, and to enforce obedience to its decisions, even as against
their judgments and consciences, then it necessarily follows as a
consequence that in all cases of conflict between the judgment of
the political State on one side and the judgment of the parent on
the other, touching any of the above-mentioned questions, it becomes
the duty of the parent to subject his own judgment to the judgment
of the State. For surely it cannot be claimed that, where the State
has the right to command, the citizen has the right to disobey the
command. But in cases of conflict between his own conscientious
judgment and the judgment of the State as to the fitness of
teachers, or books, or school companions, etc., *can* the parent,
without moral crime, subject his own judgment to that of the State?

Suppose, for example, the case of a strictly conscientious Protestant parent who, by the use of all the lights within his reach, has
come to the conclusion that the constant presence and daily reading
of the Bible in the school is one of the indispensable means of preserving the moral purity of his child; of protecting it against what
he firmly believes are the dangerous and damnable doctrines of
atheism; and of preparing it for a life of virtue, honor, and usefulness in this world, and a life of eternal happiness in the world to
come; and suppose the political State, in the exercise of its judgment,
forbids the Bible to be read in its schools, can such a parent,
without crime, send his children to such schools, believing in his
heart that by doing so he is preparing them for a life of sin and
shame, and an eternity of woe? Be it remembered that we are not
now discussing the question as to whether the Bible is or is not a
necessary or a proper book for daily use in the schools, but we are
discussing the proposition as to the State's jurisdiction to decide that
question, and to enforce obedience to its decision as against the
judgment and consciences of parents. If the political State has the
legitimate power and the rightful jurisdiction to make a binding decision on this disputed question, then whichever way it decides the
question—whether it be in favor of or against the use of the Bible
in the schools—its decision must be equally binding. For the power
to decide a disputed question, on condition that it be decided *one*
particular way and no other, simply means no power to decide the
question at all. Therefore, if the State has a rightful jurisdiction
over this question, and should decide to teach the Bible in the schools,

to the children of parents who do not believe in the Bible, such parents would have no right to complain.   For if the parental judgment and conscience are subordinate and ought to yield to the State's judgment and conscience, where would be the ground for complaint?

Again, if the State may rightfully, and without trenching upon the doctrine of religious liberty, *forbid* the teaching of the Bible in the schools, to the children of parents whose judgments and consciences demand such teaching, or may *enforce* the teaching of the Bible to the children of those whose judgments and consciences are opposed thereto, it then follows, as a matter of course, that the State must have jurisdiction to decide as to which one of all the various versions and translations of the Bible is the correct one.   In other words, it must have jurisdiction to determine which one of the various books known as the " BIBLE " is entitled to be called by that name.   Not only that, but if the State can, without encroaching upon the just liberty of conscience, decide what book *is the* Bible, and then enforce the teaching of such Bible in the schools, against the judgments and consciences of the parents of the children who are so taught, it must also have jurisdiction to decide, as between conflicting interpretations, what is the *meaning* of the various texts of the Bible, for it would be as absurd and as barren of good results to simply teach the *words* of the Bible to a child, while leaving it in ignorance as to their signification, as it would be to teach the same child to repeat, in a parrot-like manner, the words of its arithmetic or of its grammar, while allowing it to grope in darkness as to the real scientific meaning which those words were intended to convey.

But if the State has the rightful jurisdiction to decide *pro* or *con* upon the authenticity of the Scriptures, and also to interpret them for its schools, and in defiance of the judgment and consciences of parents to teach the Scriptures, *as it* interprets them, to the rising generation, does not this of itself involve the right—within the limits of its educational domain—to establish a State religion?   We can see no escape from an affirmative answer to this proposition.   In other words, we maintain that it is impossible, logically, to justify our present anti-parental State-controlled educational system, without the maintenance of principles which would justify the political State in establishing, at public expense, a State church, and teaching to the rising generation a State religion, and compelling every child to learn and practise such teachings.   If the true and just relations between the political State and its citizens are such that, in settling the question as to the *kind* of education that shall be given to the children of the latter, it is the right of the State to command and the duty of the parent to obey, then it follows that if we were citizens of some barbarous country, where the political State requires every child to learn and practice the doctrine of snake-worship, it would become our bounden duty to allow our children to be taught these vile and revolting doctrines.

Here again we insist upon its being borne in mind that we are not discussing the question as to what kind or whether any religion *ought or ought not* to be taught to children; but we are only considering the question as to whether or not it rightfully belongs to the " political State " to determine that question, and in doing so, to override the judgments and consciences of the fathers and mothers of children.

It seems to us that, from the innermost depths of every human heart, not wholly dead to the noblest impulses of man's nature, there rises up one spontaneous universal protest against this vile and monstrous usurpation of parental authority by the political State. And we firmly believe that the only thing necessary is that the people of this country, of all creeds and parties, be brought fairly and squarely face to face with this deadly foe to their liberties, so as to see the horrid monster in all its hideous deformity, and that they will then promptly stamp it out of existence. Therefore, in our humble opinion, the true and proper course to be pursued by the friends of educational reform is to keep prominently before the people as the fundamental, the vital issue, this question, namely : Shall the parent or the political State determine for a child who shall be its teacher, its companions, and what books it shall or shall not study? Let all other issues be made subordinate to this. As long as we make our chief fight on the question of Bible or no Bible, religion or no religion, division of public-school funds or no division, mixed or separate schools for girls and boys, and similar questions concerning which men will differ—and as things are, naturally and honestly differ—so long will there be contention and strife amongst the real friends of educational reform. Each of these contending factions is willing to see, and does see, the evils of an anti-parental system of education when that system strikes at his *own* rights, as he understands those rights ; but is slow to see the same evils when they only affect the rights of his neighbors, who choose to exercise *their* rights in a manner different from himself.

This should not be so. If we expect the assistance of our neighbors in our struggles for our own parental rights, we must be willing to assist those neighbors in securing *theirs*. And we must not demand, as a condition precedent, that these neighbors shall agree to exercise their parental rights just as we do ours, because this would be as intolerant and oppressive, and as opposed to parental liberty, as is the present public-school system ; or rather it would be simply a new application of the same system. It would simply be the taking of the martyred victim who is being roasted on one side, and turning the other side to the fire.

We must realize the fact that in union there is strength, and that we can only have union by being just and liberal towards each other. While standing firmly by our own rights and the rights of our children, we must realize and act upon the fact that our neighbors' rights and our neighbors' children are as dear to them as ours are to us. And however widely mistaken we may believe our neighbors to be in *their* manner of educating their children, we should remember that it is not *our* business, nor our right, to force *our* views upon them any more than it is *their* business to force *their* views upon us. It is not for *their* children but for our *own* that we shall be called upon to render an account to that God who gave them.

If, then, we would work for *union*, if we would work for success in the cause of educational liberty, let us lay aside all those side issues which every parent should settle according to his own judgment and conscience, and let us raise aloft the broad banner of parental rights and equal educational liberty, without distinction of creed, party, or calling. Under this banner we *can* conquer ; under any other I believe we shall surely fail.

CHAPTER XIV.

A NON-SECTARIAN PLATFORM OF EDUCATIONAL PRINCIPLES ALMOST UNANIMOUSLY ENDORSED BY THOSE WHO HAVE STUDIED IT.

PROPOSITIONS.

I.

Parents are bound, by the law of Nature, (each according to his ability), to properly feed, clothe, and educate their own children, and unwilling parents should be compelled, by appropriate legislation, to discharge these duties.

II.

It is a public duty to assist, at public expense, in furnishing the necessary means wherewith to properly feed, clothe, and educate children whose parents are unable to so feed, clothe, and educate them.

III.

No citizen of this State should ever be taxed for the feeding, clothing, or educating of children—not his own—whose parents are amply able to feed, clothe, and educate them.

IV.

All such parents as are neither mentally nor morally unfit to have the custody of children are entitled, and in duty bound, to select for the education of their own children schools wherein they believe that neither the teachers, the associations, nor the kind of instruction given, will seriously endanger either their health, their lives, or their morals, but will best promote their temporal and eternal welfare.

V.

Neither the State, nor any municipal or other government organized under its authority, should ever force upon the child of any parent—not legally adjudged mentally or morally unfit to discharge the duties of the parental office—any particular teacher, book, or system of religious or non-religious instruction against the conscientious objections of such parent.

VI.

Tuition, when at public expense, should embrace a good common English and business education, added to such a thorough training in one or more of the mechanic arts, or the manufacturing, domestic, or productive industries, as will best prepare youth for the practical business of self-support, but should not extend to the merely ornamental or more abstruse arts or sciences, except in a limited class of cases (to be provided for by law) as a reward for exalted merit, when coupled with a high order of talent and a special aptitude for such arts or sciences.

VII.

The whole business of educating and training the young should, like other professions, be open to private enterprise and free competition : *Provided*, That the State should establish and maintain such necessary educational institutions as private enterprise shall fail to establish and maintain ; and every parent or guardian entitled to have his or her child or ward educated at public expense should select for such purpose his own school, and the teacher or principal of such school should be paid periodically for teaching such pupil a compensation, the maximum of which shall be fixed by law, which compensation should be proportionate to the progress made by the pupil during such period of tuition in the legally appointed secular branches. Said progress to be ascertained by examiners duly elected or appointed in such manner as may be provided by law; but no religious tuition which may be given in any such school should be at public expense or subject to the supervision of said examiners.

HOW INTELLIGENT CITIZENS OF ALL CLASSES REGARD THE ABOVE PROPOSITIONS.

The friends and opponents of the foregoing propositions held a meeting in the city of Oakland on the evening of October 6, 1879, for the purpose of considering their merits. In referring to that meeting, and its action touching said propositions, a leading Oakland daily, the *Evening Tribune*, in its issue of October 10th, among other things said:

" A large audience gathered last Monday evening at the old Congregational church building, to hear the Hon. Zach. Montgomery discuss the demerits of the Public-School System of the United States. It was generally expected and hoped that the Rev. Horatio Stebbins, D. D., of San Francisco, would be present and take issue with the views advanced by Mr. Montgomery, but the reverend gentleman did not put in an appearance. Fred. M. Campbell, State Superintendent-elect, at the request of Mr. Montgomery, presided. * * * In support of the two principal opinions, namely, the pernicious influence of our present system of public instruction, and the right and duty of the parent to select and control the education of the child, as well as clothe and feed it, he advanced seven propositions, which, if carried out practically, he believed would prove vastly superior to the present system. He was frequently plied with questions, put by persons in the audience, to which he responded with alacrity. A vote was taken on the several propositions advanced by Mr. Montgomery to ascertain the sense of the audience in regard to the subject, and invariably the result showed that the speaker was sustained by the majority of his hearers."

As another evidence of the intrinsic popularity of the foregoing platform of principles it may be stated that a petition asking that a law be passed to submit said platform to a vote of the people, to test the sense of the public upon the question of so amending the California State constitution as to bring it into harmony with said platform, was endorsed by nearly every leading citizen of the cities of San Francisco and Oakland who examined the question. Among these signers were included the most prominent ministers of almost every religious denomination, as well as non-religionists of the different schools of thought.   Indeed, it is a noteworthy fact that amongst these signers was the Hon. J. F. Swift, the able and distinguised Republican nominee for Governor of California in this year of our Lord 1886. A bill was introduced in the California State Senate, in 1880, by Hon. B. F. Langford, providing for carrying out the objects of said petition.   It was referred to the Senate Committee on Education, came back with a divided report, was placed on the regular files of business, but the session—being by the constitution restricted to sixty days—expired by limitation before the bill could be reached for action.   It is a well-known fact, however, that many of the ablest and most influential members of that body stood ready to give it their cordial support.

The following are but a few of the prominent and influential names appended thereto, to wit:

Hon. JAMES T. FARLEY, (U. S. Senator.)	Hon. E. W. McKINSTRY, (Supreme Judge.)
Hon. S. B. McKEE, (Supreme Judge.)	Hon. A. M. CRANE, (Superior Judge.)

(Several other Superior Judges.)

Hon. JOHN R. GLASCOCK, (M. C.)	Hon. W. W. FOOTE, (R. R. Commissioner.)
Hon. J. F. SWIFT.	Hon. J. A. STANLEY.
Dr. S. MERRITT.	F. DELGER.
Rt. Rev. W. I. KIPP, (Episc. Bishop of Cal.)	Rev. W. A. SCOTT, (Presbyterian.)
Rev. J. K. McLEAN, (Congregationalist.)	Rev. G. S. ABBOTT, (Baptist.)
Rev. C. KENRICK, (Campbellite or Christian.)	Rev. L. HAMILTON, (Independent.)
Rev. THOS. GUARD, (Methodist.)	Rev. J. FUENDELING, (Reformed Ger. Ch.)
Rev. F. W. FISCHER, (Evangelical Ass'n.)	Rev. G. MUEHLSTEPH,(German Lutheran,)

And fourteen other prominent Protestant clergymen of San Francisco and Oakland belonging to the different denominations just enumerated.

Also Most Rev. J. S. ALEMANY, of San Francisco, and several other Roman Catholic Clergymen.

Also Dr. D. H. VIDAVER and Dr. A. J. MESSING, Jewish rabbis.

Rev. Doctor John LeConte, while president of the California State University, an eminent Presbyterian divine, after reading the author's views as expressed in " *Poison Fountain*"—without fully committing himself to these views—wrote as follows:

" *There can be no doubt that the gradual impairment and loss of parental authority and influence is one of the most serious and momentous evils which besets the American civilization.   It undermines the very foundations of the family—the essential unit of society.*"

Rev. Dr. Joseph LeConte, likewise a distinguished Presbyterian minister, a professor of the same University and a scientist and author of world-wide celebrity, addressed the writer a letter, saying, among other things: "*I fully concur with you in your view that any education which weakens the family tie strikes at the very foundation of society, and no amount of good in other directions can atone for this greatest of all evils.   I fully concur with you also in your opposition to* COMPULSORY STATE EDUCATION. *This certainly strikes at the integrity of the family, for it makes children ' the wards of the State.' I fully believe, also, that* PRIVATE SCHOOLS, *each parent choosing his own, furnish a better education, all things considered, than any public-school system."*

Rev. A. Adams, of Los Angelès, (Protestant,) writing to the author, says: *"I am struck with the similarity of our views on the school question, and bid you Godspeed in propagating your views as contained in the publication before me. I see that you, a Catholic, and I, a Protestant, are united here."*

Dr. Thomas W. Dawson, of Downey City, (non-religionist,) concludes a letter to the author as follows: *"I honestly believe that your array of facts and reasoning are simply unanswerable."*

Mr. W. D. Blackwell, of Trenton, New Jersey, wrote to the author, saying: *"I am a Presbyterian, but you and myself are in perfect harmony and accord upon this all-important school question."*

Mr. W. L. Prather, a well-known citizen and notary public of Oakland, a strict member of the Methodist Church, concluded a letter to the author as follows: *"* TRUTH *is the invincible weapon that you have so efficiently employed; a weapon that has already and will continue to work as leaven in the social and political lump until, as I trust, the whole shall become leavened."*

Hon. J. Burckhalter, of Santa Rosa, Cal., a prominent lawyer and staunch member of the Campbellite (or Christian) Church, addressed a letter to the writer on the subject of his educational fight, concluding thus: *"I hope you will have courage and go on in the good work until success shall have crowned your efforts."*

Mr. George Washington, the grand-nephew and nearest living relative of the illustrious Father of his Country, wrote to the author from Center View, Mo., April 13th, 1880:

" Please send me a copy of your celebrated pamphlet against public schools.   I have read copious extracts from the same, but want a copy in full for re-reading and reference. It will keep. I am as much opposed to the system as yourself, but have not the ability to express my objections as clearly, pointedly, and forcibly as you have yours.
" Respectfully,
" GEORGE WASHINGTON."

TWO MOST SIGNIFICANT FACTS—SUBSTANTIAL ENDORSEMENTS BY A CONGRE-
GATIONAL STATE COUNCIL AND A PRESBYTERIAN STATE SYNOD.

It is well known that the Congregational clergymen of California are mostly New England men, and it is equally well known that such of them as have investigated the subject are almost, if not quite, a unit in their endorsement of our educational platform. As an evidence of this, in 1879 a California State Council of Congregational clergymen convened in San Francisco appointed Rev. Dr. J. K. McLean, one of its most distinguished members—and a signer of the above-mentioned petition embodying our educational platform—to prepare a document touching the school question. At an adjourned meeting, which convened in Oakland October 6th, 1880, the Rev. Doctor made a carefully-prepared report, entitled—

"THE PROPER LIMITS OF STATE EDUCATION."

This report was in substantial accord with the principles set forth in said platform.

In proof of this, only a few quotations will be necessary. For example, this report says:

" *The State should limit itself in the field of education as it does in all the other fields it occupies; that is, it may provide, and ought to provide, elementary teaching for those who would not otherwise get it; but only on the same ground on which it provides bread and clothing and shelter and medicine for those who would not otherwise get them.*" Again,

" *State education should be limited certainly to what is known as common-school instruction; possibly to the three elementary branches, reading, writing, and arithmetic.*" Again,

" A rapidly increasing number of people in the churches, perceiving the impossibility of harmonizing opinions into any sort of working agreement as to *what* shall be taught, as to *how* it shall be taught, and by what kind of *persons* it shall be taught, are arriving at the conclusion that the *wiser* way, the *juster* way, the far more satisfactory way, will be no longer to put our education money into a common fund, except so far as to guard the State against utter illiteracy; but for the party of each opinion to be allowed to keep its higher educational money in its own hands, and to expend it in such manner as shall seem to itself good. This will be for the interest of State harmony no less than for the interest of education itself. *Then the Catholic father can enjoy his indefeasible right to educate his child after his own judgment and conscience; the infidel father can enjoy his indefeasible right, and the Protestant Christian his.*" Again, the Rev. Doctor's report says:

" As matters now stand, the non-religionist party are, in some of our States, oppressors. They are refusing the religionist liberty of conscience as touching a most important and far-reaching matter. The non-religionist exacts money from the religionist for purposes of a common education, and then refuses the religionist any voice or influence in the management of that education. For me, a religionist, believing that a certain moral culture should be joined to all mental culture; believing, indeed, that the two cannot by any possibility be separated; believing that the absence of positive moral culture is equivalent to a culture in *im*morality—just as the absence of certain elements in the atmosphere leaves it poisonously noxious—for me to insist that some appliances for moral culture shall be included in our common system of education is bigotry.   There must be two taxes and one voice. I can pay, but can have no say. There is no bigotry in the non-religionist having what *he* wants at the common expense, but for the religionist to claim some allowance for his wants is the essence of bigotry.

So great is the divergence of opinion as to systems of education, so impossible of remediation does this divergency appear to be, that very many of us are beginning to think that the only peaceable and harmonious way must be to follow the example set in early days in the matter of State religion—for the State simply to protect all parties in their opinions, and relegate to each parent the business of providing his children with such higher education as his judgment may suggest or his conscience dictate. *The same principle, precisely, appears to underlie both matters, that of church and State, and that of school and State.*"

This able report of the Rev. Doctor's was promptly adopted and published to the world as expressing the views of the Council. Subsequently, a Presbyterian State Synod, held in San Francisco, appointed Rev. Dr. Scott, one of its ablest members, (who was also one of the signers of our said petition), to prepare a report on the same subject. His report, when prepared, was also in perfect harmony with said petition and with the views proclaimed by the Congregational Council. Rev. Dr. Scott's report was also adopted by nearly, if not quite, a unanimous vote of the Synod.

The important significance of the action thus taken by these two highly-intelligent and influential bodies of men in favor of parental rights and equal liberty in educational matters can scarcely be overestimated.

It would be easy to fill page after page with the endorsements from distinguished Protestant, Jewish, and non-religious sources, but it is now in order to show that our non-sectarian platform of educational principles is as acceptable to intelligent and fair-minded Catholics as it is to non-Catholics.

For example: Archbishop Seghers, writing from Portland, Oregon, March 26th, 1883, among other things, says:

" The logic with which you grapple with the educational prob-
" lem is irresistible, and, as the champion of the only system of edu-
" cation that can be reared on principles of truth and justice, you
" are simply admirable. When I read your thoughts I feel that
" they are the outcome of long, careful, patient study and of con-
" scientious convictions."

Bishop Grace, of St. Paul, Minnesota, in February, 1881, writing to the author upon the subject of his magazine, then being published, among other things, said :

" You have judged wisely in making your magazine non-sectarian
" and appealing to the common sense and calm judgment of the
" American people at large.   I have long since been convinced that
" this was the proper course from the beginning.   By making the
" movement appear a strictly Catholic movement, upon Catholic
" grounds, *we forfeited the sympathy and co-operation of the*
" *communities of other creeds, and by our over-heated zeal we*
" *alienated from us the liberal-minded among our better citizens*
" *in general.*"

Subsequently, the same eminent prelate wrote to the author, saying :

" If you need any words of mine to encourage you in the course you are pursuing, you have them from my heart.   Every day convinces me more and more that the ground you have taken in defence of the rights of the family against the encroachments of the State is really the ground upon which the opposition to the State school system should have been based from the beginning.   Natural rights, as involved in this question, no legitimate Government will infringe, or allow to be infringed, upon due proof.   The law of majorities, the *vox populi*, has no weight against the claims of natural family rights."

More than a dozen other distinguished American bishops and archbishops, including Archbishop Elder, of Cincinnati ; Bishop Spalding, of Peoria ; Bishop Ryan, of Buffalo, N. Y.; Bishop Gilmoure, of Cleveland, Ohio ; Bishop Marty, of Dakota ; Bishop Seidenbush, of Minnesota ; Bishop Fink, of Leavenworth ; Bishop Hogan, of Kansas City, and all the Pacific Coast bishops, have joined in the substantial endorsement of our aforesaid educational platform ; and, last but not least, the great Cardinal Manning, of England, concluded an article on the school question (published in the *Nineteenth Century* for April, 1883) by saying that he could not do better than repeat the above letter of Bishop Grace, commending, as we have just seen, in the strongest terms the author's position.

The truth is that *wherever*, and *whenever*, and by *whomsoever*, our platform of educational principles has been studied in connection with our compilation of criminal statistics, it has been almost invariably endorsed.

At least we feel warranted in saying that wherever the school question has been carefully considered from the stand-point presented in these pages, the number of those who endorse our platform, compared with the number who reject it, stands in the proportion of not less than

SIX TO ONE.

As a fair test of the truth of this proposition it may be stated that, in the month of June, 1881, it was announced in the Oakland papers that the writer would deliver two pay lectures in Cameron Hall, Oakland, to wit: on the evenings of Friday and Saturday, July 1st and 2d; the first lecture to be in answer to the question, " Which of the two is the more plausible theory, namely, that man is an improved monkey, or that the monkey is an improved man?" and printed on the backs of the tickets of admission was the following, as indicating the programme and the nature of the subject for Saturday evening's lecture, to wit:

CHANCE FOR A PRIZE.

On the evening of the second lecture a prize, consisting of twenty-five per cent. of the net proceeds of both lectures, will be awarded to the person present who shall, in the fewest words, not exceeding one hundred in number, furnish in writing the best original answer, with the chief reasons therefor, to the following question, to wit:

In cases where, on the one hand, the judgment and conscience of a proper parent, fit to be guardian of his own child, and on the other, the judgment and conscience of the school officials and of the general public differ, irreconcilably, as to whether said child, when of school age, can, with safety to its health, its life, or its morals, be educated in such schools as the public has provided for that purpose, whose judgment and conscience ought to control—that of the parent or that of the school officials and the general public?

Said award will be made immediately before the second lecture, by an umpire to be chosen by the competing respondents, whose answers must all be handed to the doorkeeper by $7\frac{1}{2}$ o'clock.

The answer taking the prize will constitute the subject of the second lecture.

The lectures came off as appointed, and seven competing answers to the foregoing questions were handed in.   Hon. J. C. Martin was elected umpire to pass upon the merits of the several answers; and upon his request to have two assistants to aid him in arriving at a correct conclusion, he was authorized by a unanimous vote to select such assistants, whereupon he selected Dr. D. Skilling and Mr. John Lynch.   After a careful examination and comparison of the various answers, the preference was, by unanimous consent, given to that of Hon. A. R. Redman, which is as follows:

The judgment of the parent must control, because—
1st. The instinctive love and mutual affection of parent and child

afford assurances of protection for the latter, and are elements which cannot be alienated, transferred, or divested.

2d. These natural instincts and the duty of the parent to support the child, the right to enjoy its services and companionship, cannot co-exist with a higher authority resting elsewhere to " educate " it, without an *irrepressible conflict* subversive of these natural and in-alienable duties and obligations, which are based upon the laws of nature and of God.

(Signed)   A. R. REDMAN.

The following are the other six competing answers, with the sig-natures of their respective authors appended :

The judgment of the school officials and the general public (should control), " because the school officials and general public, being equally interested in all the children, decide unselfishly."

2d. The motto of the school officials and general public is, The greatest good to the greatest number.

3d. The school which the public has provided is the result of the aggregated wisdom and virtue of the State or community.

4th. The school officials and general public believe that virtue must be brought in contact with vice both to strengthen virtue and to weaken vice.

5th. The public school proposes a sufficiently high but general development for all.

(Signed)   J. C. LAWSON.

The judgment of the parent (should control), because he " *is a proper parent fit to be guardian of his own child*," none feeling the same interest in the child as the parent, and none so able to form its character.

2d. Because the parent is directly responsible to God for the proper training of the child, and no one other than the parent should have control or assume the responsibility that rests only on the parent.

(Signed)   W. L. PRATHER.

A proper parent should control the education of his child. His judgment concerning the mental, physical, and moral needs of his own offspring, with whom he is in daily contact, must be better than that of paid officials, who, in handling an incongruous mass of immature minds, can know little of each individual temperament, and in many instances cares less. The sound judgment of the par-ent admitted, his conscience would naturally dictate to him his duty. He should place his child under the best moral and social influence, and of them he is the best judge.

(Signed)   J. L. ABELL.

The parent, (should control), otherwise would he violate the law guaranteeing liberty, and providing that no citizen should be de-prived of liberty except by due process. Naturally the parent is the best judge, knowing the child best, and he would from every consideration care most, and certainly the community's real interests are never jeopardized by the true interest of one of its citizens. The great interest of the child is not considered by the people or their repre-sentatives—the greatest and best interest of the soul. The parent looks to this, if a proper parent.

(Signed)   J. C. KENDRICK, M. D.

____

God has made it both the right and the duty of the parent to sup-port and educate his child, nor can any power justly deprive him of this right or release him from this duty. The duty and the right are inseparable.

If the State can of right prescribe the schools and education, it can of right prescribe its religion. This would be anti-American and subversive of our free institutions.

(Signed)   H. H. HENDRIX.

____

None should come between my child and me, or dictate how I should educate or raise it; for my heart alone will grieve if false teachings lead it astray, and my soul alone is responsible to the eternal God for His charge. My money is *mine*, and it is but just that I use it for my child's interest in schools I approve.

Education without religion is as bad as total ignorance. Better a godly citizen than a classical knave ; political mills are not places wherein my child can learn honesty, morality, and virtue.

(Signed)   M. E. L.,
375 Fourth Street, City.

It will be observed that there is nothing either in the question itself, or in any of the foregoing answers, in the least tinged with what is usually called sectarian bias. Six of the competing parties were either Protestants or non-religionists, and two of the umpires were Protestants and one Catholic. Taking both the seven com-petitors and the three umpires, they make ten in all, and represent almost that many shades of religious belief; and yet—as will be seen by reading these answers, and the names of the umpires appended to the award—they stood solid for parental rights, nine against one. It is our solemn conviction that whenever this ques-tion can be brought squarely before the people, so that they can vote upon it understandingly, more than nine to one will vote against this monstrous usurpation, whereby parents are robbed of their natural and God-given rights in so sacred a matter as that of select-ing schools for their own children.

There is but one of the foregoing answers upon which we deem it necessary to comment, because each of the others seems to embody, in different forms of expression, the same sound doctrine as that contained in the one to which the umpires gave the preference. The answer to which we cannot subscribe is that of Mr. Lawson.

He maintains that where there is a conflict between the judgment and conscience of a proper parent on the one side, and the judgment and conscience of the school officials and the general public on the other, as to whether a child can with safety to its health, its life, and its morals be sent to such school as the public has established, the judgment of the school officials and the general public should control. And his reasons are: First, "because the school officials and the general public, being equally interested in all the children, decide unselfishly."

Now, in the first place, we deny the truth of this statement, because, unless the school officials are all old bachelors, or otherwise childless persons, it is impossible for them to be "*equally interested in all the children.*" In other words, it is in the very nature of things impossible for the parents of children to feel no more interest in the proper education of their own than in that of their neighbor's children or the children of strangers. Should the school officials happen to be childless persons, it may then be possible for them to feel "equally interested in all the children;" but, in such a case, we contend that as a rule they could not feel that degree of interest in *any* of the children which the person *ought* to feel whose duty it is to select a school for the protection of the health, the life, and the morals of a child. To show, in a few words, the utter fallacy of Mr. Lawson's first argument, let us suppose that instead of a young child, whose health and morals are at stake, we take the case of a young swine, whose health and life alone are involved, and we will ask the question whether that young swine ought for safety to be left to the care of its own mother, who feels for it an instinctive affection that no other swine can, or whether it would be better to take it from its own mother and intrust it to the tender mercies of a herd of strange hogs? Most unquestionably, according to Mr. Lawson's first proposition, the pig would be better taken care of by the general herd, because they would take just as much interest in that as they would in any other strange pig. Yet we venture the opinion that were Mr. Lawson engaged in the business of raising hogs instead of raising babies, he would rather trust the care and management—and educational control, if you please— of his young pigs to their own mothers than to any or all the other swine in Christendom; not certainly upon the ground that she felt an equal interest in all the pigs in the country as in her own, but upon the very ground that she did not, because if those affections, and that interest which ought to be lavished upon a dozen of her own, were divided in equal parts between *them* and a thousand others it is very certain that her own would suffer. The God of nature, in His infinite wisdom, has ordained that the educational control of the child should be entrusted to those who feel for it far more than such a *general* interest as is equally applicable to all the children in the community. He who is to select a school for a child with a view of preserving its health, its life, and its morals, ought to be a person who loves such child with a parent's love ; and nobody but a parent can do that. He ought to be a person who has a parent's opportunities of knowing both the mental and physical peculiarities of the child, because a strong, robust child might with safety endure a school atmosphere which would be certain death to another of a more delicate constitution.

Again, a cross, stern, and severe teacher, such as would be an absolute necessity for a certain class of rough, uncouth, incorrigible youths, would often so unnerve the child of a timid, sensitive nature as to destroy its health, inspire it with horror for the very name of school, and place it beyond the range of possibility for it to learn.

Again, he who is to control the child's education ought to feel, as only a parent can feel, that his own individual happiness, as well as that of the child, will largely depend upon the kind of teachers and companions he selects for such a child. He should feel that either the death or moral ruin, or the unfitting of such child for any honest pursuit within its reach, will result in an irreparable disaster to *himself* as well as the child.

As suggested in one of the foregoing answers, the child in the hands of its parents is a sacred trust from the Almighty, and He has imposed, even in this life, terrible penalties upon the violators of this trust. In the language of an immutable law, which He has indelibly written on the parental heart, He has plainly said to every father and mother to whom He has given a child: " *This* child is *My* handiwork. It bears *My* image. It is a jewel more precious than all the treasures of earth. At thy solicitation I intrust it to thy keeping, in order that thou mayest feed and clothe and train it up in the way it should go. I charge thee to shield it from sickness and death, and the still more terrible curse of crime against My laws."

In order to make the faithful discharge of this trust a pleasing duty, rather than an irksome task, the Almighty has given to you—fathers and mothers—a fond and ardent love for *your own child*, such as other parents may bear towards *their* children, but such as no other human being in this world can ever bear towards *yours*. He has, moreover, implanted in the heart of *your* child the seeds of filial love for YOU, such as other children may feel for their *own* parents, but such as none but *your* children can ever feel for *you.*

He has likewise sealed and confirmed your parental authority over your child by commanding it, under the severest penalties, to *honor and obey you*, its father and mother. Thus armed with a God-given authority, and charged with the God-imposed duty of selecting for your *own* child a proper school, if, in deference to the wishes, or in obedience to the commands, of the outer world, you *allow* your child to be hurried to an untimely grave or plunged into the polluting mire of iniquity, it is not the *outer world*—the usurper of your sacred office—but *you, yourself*, together with your child, who must chiefly suffer the terrible consequences of such usurpation.

Yours are the sleepless nights that must be spent in watching by the bedside of your sick or dying child, and yours the bleeding heart that must writhe in agony as you look upon the lifeless form of that beautiful cherub who has fallen a victim to the poisoned air of an over-crowded school-room, or other death-producing cause, to which, in defiance of your own solemn convictions of duty, you have exposed it, because the public-school officials demanded the sacrifice ; or worse.

Still, should your idolized son, or your once spotless daughter, in consequence of the false maxims or bad example of an immoral teacher, or the vile associations of wicked school-mates, become a burning disgrace to your name, it is *you* who will have to hang your head in unutterable shame and confusion, while the *very persons* at whose bidding you have allowed your child's mind and heart to be poisoned, and its doom of degradation and misery sealed for time and eternity, will shun you as they would shun a leper ; and they will point you out to the passing stranger as an " old fellow who has a son in the penitentiary," or " a daughter in a house of ill-fame." And on the great accounting day, what excuse can you frame for so base a betrayal of your high trust?

Mr. Lawson's second reason assigned in support of his theory, that the parent's judgment and conscience ought to yield to the judgment and conscience of the public-school officials and the general public, is " because the motto of the school officials and the general public is, The greatest good to the greatest number."

Now, if we have been successful—as we think we have—in showing that God Almighty has so formed human nature, and so established the relations between parent and child, that, as a general rule, the greatest good both of children and parents requires that the parental judgment and conscience should control in the matter of selecting schools for children, then we think that the said second reason is already fully answered.

Mr. Lawson's third reason is that the school which the public has provided is the result of the aggregated wisdom and virtue of the State or community. We think that a little reflection, and a careful inspection of facts and figures, such as we have carefully collected from the United States Census Reports and placed before our readers, will convince any candid mind that, as a general proposition, " the school which the public has provided" comes much nearer being " the result of the aggregated" folly and vice of " the State or community" than it does to being its aggregated wisdom and virtue.

We would, moreover, inquire what does, or can, the aggregated wisdom of the State know about the individual tastes, dispositions, inclinations, mental, moral, and physical peculiarities of your little seven or ten-year-old girl, whose very existence is not known to more than one out of ten thousand of the voters who are supposed to represent " the aggregated wisdom of the State?" And who, we ask, if in search of knowledge touching those very characteristics and peculiarities of the child which ought to be considered when selecting the school wherein her whole future life is to be shaped, would not infinitely rather consult the father and mother than all " the aggregated wisdom" of the outside world? We would much rather trust to the individual wisdom of a mother goose for the proper management and training of her own goslings than to the aggregated wisdom of all the other geese in Christendom.

But Mr. Lawson's fourth reason for depriving parents of the right to exercise their own judgments and consciences in the matter of selecting schools for their children, although in perfect harmony both with the theory and the practical workings of our present public-school system, is certainly a most startling one. He says: " The school officials and general public believe that virtue must be brought in contact with vice both to strengthen virtue and to weaken vice." If this be sound philosophy, then should every young man who aspires to a reputation for strict and sterling integrity first serve his time in the company of pick-pockets, burglars, forgers, counterfeiters, garroters, thieves, and robbers. And no young lady should be considered strong in the virtue of purity until she has first waltzed with a thousand lascivious rakes and served an apprenticeship in a bawdy-house.

It is evident that Pope, the poet, was not versed in the Lawsonian

philosophy, or he never would have written those oft-quoted lines
saying:

> " Vice is a monster of so frightful mien
> As to be hated needs but to be seen;
> Yet seen too oft, familiar with her face,
> We first endure, then pity, then embrace."

Neither did Lord Byron have the least idea of the great advantage which a virtuous boy derives from vile associations, nor how
easy it is for a young lad to grow strong in virtue amidst scenes of
vice, when he penned the words—

> "Ah vice! how soft are thy voluptuous ways!
> When boyish blood is mantling, who can 'scape
> The fascination of thy magic gaze?

We wonder if it was because of his contact with vice and the
vicious enemies of our Saviour that the Apostle Peter became so
strong in virtue that at the voice of a servant handmaid he denied
his Divine Master and swore that he knew not the man?

As stated in another chapter, a committee of Massachusetts ladies,
after visiting the public schools of their State a short time ago, made
a report, declaring " that teachers almost universally complain of the
prevalence of lying, stealing, profanity, and impurity among their
scholars." Now, if this statement is true, and if Mr. Lawson's
philosophy is sound, what a splendid place a Massachusetts public
school must be in which to strengthen and give, as it were, the fin-
ishing touch to the pious education of a virtuous youth. If Mr.
Lawson's doctrine—which, after all, is simply the doctrine whereon
rests the present anti-parental public-school system—is to be the set-
tled doctrine on educational questions in this country, what becomes of
the liberty of conscience? If the public and not the parental judgment and conscience must determine as to the fitness of the school
for each individual child, suppose that the people of some religious
denomination should one of these days obtain a predominating
influence in elections, and should, in obedience to the public conscience, force the teaching of their religion upon all children, in
utter disregard of the dictates of the parental conscience of thousands of unbelievers in the popular religion; would anybody deny
that this would be a violation of the principle of religious liberty?
And yet is it any more a violation of religious liberty to force a
child to study the doctrines and principles of a religion, against
which the consciences of its parents protest, than to force that same
child into associations with immoral teachers and vile companions
which these same parents conscientiously believe will be a thousand

times more injurious to the child than the most objectionable religious teachings?   In this connection there is one thought that
sometimes fills us with amazement with reference to the action of
a vast number of people of all creeds, and it is this: While they
are particularly, and we may say properly, careful to guard against
the teaching of any religion in the public schools which may tend
to estrange their children from their own, there is, as a rule, comparatively little heed paid by any class of religionists to the vicious,
degrading, and criminal principles and practices of either teachers
or school companions, by means of which millions of those children
not only lose all faith in the creeds of their parents, but learn to
despise the very name of religion, and finally leave school both
confirmed atheists and hardened criminals.   Our readers will
understand that this remark is not made in any sectarian sense, for
we believe in our heart that it applies with nearly equal force to
Catholics, Protestants, and Jews.

Judging from their actions and their non-actions, it would really
seem that there is a vast number of professing religionists, clergymen
as well as laymen, who think it matters but very little if children do
go to hell, provided they get there by some other road than by the
way of a wrong religion.   For our own part we do sincerely believe
that our ungodly and anti-parental public-school education is doing
far more to-day to people the devil's dominions than all the false
religions in the world.

THE ACTION OF THE PRESIDENT AND SENATE WITH REFERENCE TO THE WRITER'S APPOINTMENT AND CONFIRMATION.

The bitter and unrelenting war so recently waged against the
writer's appointment and confirmation as U. S. Assistant Attorney-General because of his views on the educational question is
well known to the public, and the utter failure of that bigoted
and fanatical war to accomplish its purpose is equally well known.
The Senatorial discussions touching the immediate subject of his
confirmation having been conducted in secret session, the writer
has, of course, no means of knowing, except from generally-ac-
cepted report, what was said or done either by his friends in
order to secure his confirmation or by his opponents in order to
prevent it.   It is generally understood, however, that the matter
was twice referred to the Judiciary Committee and twice reported
upon adversely by a strictly partisan vote.   It was also generally
understood and never—to the writer's knowledge—denied that, after
the refutation of the anonymous slander quoted by Mr. Senator In-

galls during the debate on the "Blair" bill, the only objection openly urged against him was because of his views on the school question, as set forth in his little pamphlet, "DROPS FROM THE POISON FOUNTAIN."

It was in view of *this* objection that—as stated in our introductory remarks—we sent a copy of said pamphlet to every member of the Senate, accompanied by a request in each case that if the Senator to whom it was addressed could find anything therein tending to prove the author's unfitness for the office he held he might be notified of the fact. No such notification was ever received, and the fact that his confirmation followed soon after the distribution of said pamphlets, while it does not prove that a majority of the Senators or any of them endorse the writer's views on the school question, it *does* prove that a majority of the members of that august body, including a number of broad-minded Republicans, could find nothing in said views to warrant them in ostracizing from official position the man who proclaimed them. And this of itself can only be regarded as a most magnificent triumph of intelligence over ignorance; of truth over falsehood; and of true liberality over bigotry, fanaticism, and proscription. With these barriers broken down, if the principles we proclaim are just and right they are sure to prevail. But if they are wrong we do not desire their success.

CHAPTER XV.

A VITAL QUESTION FOR PUBLIC-SCHOOL TEACHERS.

IN a work entitled the "Daily Public School," published by Lippincott in 1866, at pages 77–78 we find it stated that "*the most frequent failures noticed in the reports are in matters of discipline or government. And this is perhaps the most difficult of all others to remedy.*"

The author then goes on to attribute this failure of discipline in the public schools to a want of capacity in the public-school teachers to govern pupils.

We have no doubt but that in many cases there is amongst our public-school teachers a lack of governing capacity. But we maintain that, as a general rule, the want of discipline amongst our common-school pupils arises chiefly from causes inherent in the very system under which they are being educated. These causes consist chiefly in a lack of legitimate authority, and are of such a nature that the very best of teachers are powerless to remove or control them.

We maintain the principle laid down by Blackstone, and recognized by all moral and religious writers, as well as every lawyer worthy of the name, that all authority is from God, and that to fathers and mothers has He entrusted so much authority as is necessary for the government of their own children.

The Divine command, which says " Honor thy father and mother," was engraved upon the heart of every child of Adam long before it was either written upon tables of stone or thundered from the heights of Sinai. The law requiring children to obey their own parents need not to be learned, for it is *innate* in their very natures. It is born with them ; it is a part of themselves, and instinctively becomes their rule of conduct before their young minds are capable of even the simplest process of reasoning. Just as the young lamb naturally hearkens to the voice of its own mother, while heedless of the babel-like bleatings of a thousand other ewes of the same flock, so does the young babe—unless deterred by the folly or wickedness of those who called it into being—instinctively recognize and obey the parental command, despite the jarring and discordant notes of ten thousand protesting tongues.

The God of nature has so wisely and so beneficently connected the path of parental duty on the one side with the path of filial obedience on the other that it is next to impossible for fathers and mothers to faithfully pursue the former without leading their children into the latter.

Until taught suspicion by repeated contact with a selfish, deceitful, and treacherous world, children are by nature of a trustful, confiding disposition, and, as a rule, parents have only to prove themselves worthy of the confidence of their little ones in order to insure that confidence.

The child's *earliest* impressions are the *deepest*, the strongest, and the *most* enduring ; and *these* impressions are, as a rule, *derived from its own father and mother*.

By the merciful dispensations of Divine Providence the new-born babe, in the very dawn of its infant consciousness, finds itself sweetly reposing in the arms and nestling in the bosom of a loving mother, or gleefully dangling upon the knee of a doting father. Out of its mother's breast it draws the very sustenance of life, whilst from her ever-watchful eye beams the first genial sunlight of human sympathy

and affection capable of warming into life and activity the *love* germs
which Divinity has planted in its pure and innocent heart. And who
does not know that *love* constitutes the great motive power of obedience? Did not HE, who is the very source and fountain of truth,
say " If you *love* me you will keep my commandments?" And what
is easier or sweeter or more gratifying to human nature than the doing of that which most pleases the one who is the most beloved?
And who on earth has more numerous or stronger claims upon the
love of a child than its own father and mother, provided they discharge the duties of father and mother?

In view of these and kindred considerations, it becomes obvious
that, as a rule, nobody in the wide world stands in so favorable a
position to command the obedience of a child as do its own parents,
because nobody else is in a position to establish so perfect a title to
the love and gratitude of the child; nor has anybody else the same
natural right to be honored and obeyed by a child, in all things lawful, as have its own father and mother.

Therefore, the school teacher who expects a willing and cheerful
obedience at the hands of a pupil should come invested with an
authority which belongs alone to the father and mother of such pupil,
and with which they alone have the power to clothe him. Such *is*
the authority which parents confer upon the teachers of *private*
schools whom they select for the extremely delicate and important
duty of educating and training their children.

But such is not the authority which the teacher of a public school
wields over his pupils.

On the contrary, as the law provides and as the courts have repeatedly decided,[1] the teacher derives his authority over his pupils
not from their respective parents but from the political State. It is
by and under the State's authority that rules are made both for
teachers and pupils; it is by and under State authority, and in defiance alike of teachers, parents, and pupils, that particular books
are used and others proscribed; and it is in obedience to State authority, and not of their own free-will and choice, that parents are
compelled to send their children to these schools under pain of
absolutely forfeiting all money paid by them for public-school purposes, besides hazarding numberless prosecutions and fines for a
failure to send them.[2]

Therefore, when the pupil of a common school is commanded by

---

[1] See California State Superintendent's Biennial Report for 1864–'65, and judicial decision there cited.

[2] See statute passed by the California Legislature March 28, 1874, (quoted *ante*.)

his teacher to be punctual in his attendance, to read a particular book, to devote himself to a particular study, to refrain from this or that forbidden practice, he does not and cannot regard such command as bearing the seal of parental authority. On the contrary, he feels and knows in his heart of hearts—however imperfectly he may be able to express that knowledge—that such command comes from the political State, the usurper of the parental prerogative, the violator of parental right, and the destroyer of parental authority.

He feels and knows that his own father, however intelligent, honorable, and upright he may be, has had no more voice in determining who should be his teacher, what classes he should attend, what books he should use, or what rules he should obey, than had the meanest and most besotted drunkard, ruffian, and rake that ever polluted the precincts of a tippling-shop with his vile presence.

If, then, it is true that *love* is the great incentive to obedience, what sort of motive shall we bring to bear upon the minds and hearts of the pupils of our anti-parental common schools in order to incite them to obey their rules and observe their discipline?

Amid the repeated clashings and conflicts between home thought, home instruction, and home discipline on one side, and common-school thought, common-school instruction, and common-school discipline on the other, such as the pupils of our common schools are necessarily doomed either to witness or to encounter in one shape or another, it must soon become apparent to the intellect of the dullest of these pupils that his teachers, however intelligent, learned, and virtuous they may be, are not at liberty to follow either the dictates of their own judgments and consciences, or to respect the wishes of its parents, either in prescribing the particular books it shall study, the companions with whom it shall associate, the rules it shall obey, or the punishment it shall undergo as the penalty of its disobedience.

The child soon learns the lesson taught by Mr. John Swett in his Biennial Report as California State Superintendent of Public Instruction in 1864, namely: That

" *The vulgar impression that parents have a legal right to dictate to teachers is entirely erroneous.*" That
" *There is no privity of contract between the parents of pupils to be sent to school and the school-master. That the latter is employed and paid by the town, and to them only is he responsible on his contract.*" That
" *The only persons who have a legal right to give orders to the teacher are his employers, namely, the committee in some States and in others the directors or trustees.*" And that

"If his conduct is approved of by his employers, the parents have no remedy against him or them."

Excellent teachers of common schools often complain that their pupils disregard their commands, and that when punished for so doing their parents get angry and use harsh and insulting language towards them.

To the common-school teacher who does not stop to trace effects back to their legitimate causes, it of course looks very unreasonable that parents should get angry and become abusive and insulting to them because of their having inflicted merited punishment upon their children. But a moment's reflection will show that the anger of such parents is not after all so unreasonable as might at first blush appear.

Before any one can be properly entitled to punish another two things are essentially necessary, namely :

First, the punishment should be just ; and,

Secondly, it should come from one having authority to administer it.

It is a well-settled principle of law that the killing of the very worst murderer in the world by one not properly authorized to inflict the death penalty, even after such criminal has been tried, convicted, and sentenced to death, would itself be murder. Not, indeed, because the murderer did not deserve killing, but because his slayer had no authority to kill him.

But it is as natural with an individual as it is with a Government to resent any unauthorized invasion by another of his personal jurisdiction and authority. Even the owner of a dumb brute dislikes to have it punished by another without his individual consent. Hence, he who kicks his neighbor's dog, without asking that neighbor's permission, need not be surprised if he receive another kick in return, although the dog may have richly deserved the punishment.

Is it, then, surprising if parents revolt at the idea of having their little children, their own flesh and blood and bone, beat and bruised and mangled, not by *their* authority, but by the authority of the *town?*

Even well-merited chastisement, when inflicted on a child, cannot have its proper effect unless the child is made to realize the fact that he who authorized such punishment did so in obedience to the dictates of a loving heart.

But where is there a child that God has blessed with an affectionate father and mother that is so stupid as not to know that for *it* the most loving heart on earth is the parental heart? Yet, whenever the common-school teacher either spares the rod or lays on the lash, he does so, as we have seen, not by parental authority, but in obedience to the requirements and at the dictation of the " town."

Here, then, is the first great and insurmountable obstacle which even the very best teachers necessarily encounter in their efforts to enforce discipline in a common school, namely, the wrong source whence they derive their jurisdiction and authority over their pupils.

And it is easy to see that this difficulty can never be remedied under the present system ; because the system itself is at war with the unchanging and unchangeable laws of nature and nature's God, commanding children to love, honor, and obey their fathers and mothers, but not commanding them to obey those who wrongfully usurp their fathers' and mothers' places.

Another and kindred difficulty which bars the way to discipline, and defies the best intended efforts to maintain order in the common schools—even by the best of teachers—arises in part from a want of that degree of freedom and independence which would allow the teacher to hearken to the dictates of his own judgment. On every side the principals and teachers of the common schools find themselves crippled, haltered, and hampered in a thousand ways. They are hampered by statutory school laws ; hampered by State boards of education ; hampered by county boards and by city boards ; hampered by superintendents ; hampered by the ceaseless criticisms, fault-findings, and backbitings of jealous rivals, who have either been superseded by them in their positions as teachers, or by whom they are themselves in danger of being superseded ; and hampered by the ceaseless dread of offending in the person of some influential ward politician, or some purse-proud upstart parent who demands special privileges for his precious scion.

In the first place, as just stated, the teacher is hampered by the statutory school laws in a manner to defy discipline.

For example : We all know how fatal to the discipline of a school is the perpetual presence of even a few rude, unruly boys. And yet the law leaves the teachers and even the principals of public schools utterly helpless so far as any power of their own is concerned to rid their schools of the vilest young imps that ever breathed.

For instance, we have a statute giving to school directors or trustees the sole power to exclude "filthy or vicious children from school."

Under the operation of this statute, no difference how unruly, disobedient, or vile a pupil may be, nor how destructive to the discipline of the school his pernicious example may prove, still it depends upon the *trustees*, and upon them alone, to either rid the school of his presence or not at their option.

As a fair illustration of the disciplinary workings of this machine system of common schools, we shall here repeat an anecdote related by the inimitable Gail Hamilton, at page 109 of her spicy little book entitled

" OUR COMMON-SCHOOL SYSTEM."

" Not long ago," says the authoress, " a boy of the third class, in a school thoroughly furnished with all the officers required by our efficient *system*, was eating candy in school, and was directed by his teacher to throw it into the waste-basket. He complied at once, re-marking, as he passed her, that she was ' a d—d fool,' in tones loud enough to be heard throughout the room. The teacher sent him home, and appealed to the superintendent of schools, who replied that 'had she suspended the boy he could do something, but now did not like to interfere, and would rather the committee should set-tle it.' The committee were consulted, the boy remaining in the school the while, and the committee held up the discipline of the school and the beauties of the ' system ' by the startling assurance to the boy that for the next offence, of whatever nature, he was to be ' sent to me !' "

Now, it can require but very little calm reflection to convince even the dullest intellect how utterly impossible it would be for the best teacher in America to maintain the discipline of his or her school under circumstances like these.

By thus impliedly excusing the boy for calling his teacher a fool, this committee virtually joined in reiterating the odious and insult-ing epithet, and thereby licensed every other pupil in the school to manifest their regard for her and her authority in a similar manner.

If it be said that this was only an isolated case, we reply that, while this particular case may be an isolated one, the spirit of in-subordination to which it owes its origin is not by any means an isolated or an exceptional one, as the above quotation from " The Daily Common School" clearly indicates, and as the daily expe-rience of our public-school teachers throughout the country abun-dantly attests.

The reasons why teachers cannot, as a rule, rely upon school trustees to actively and cordially second their efforts to maintain the discipline of their schools have already been dwelt upon; but a few more words in this connection on that subject may not be out of place.

As already intimated, it very often happens that school trustees do not have, and are not required or expected by those to whom they are chiefly indebted for their positions to have, any special fitness for their offices aside from an unswerving fidelity to their friends, coupled with the necessary capacity to render themselves serviceable to those who have served them. Let us take, then, for example the case of the boy spoken of by Gail Hamilton, who had called his lady teacher a fool. The boy's conduct is reported to the superintendent, whose duty it is supposed to be to protect the teacher against insult and to maintain the discipline of the school. But it so happens that this boy's father is an influential ward politician. He belongs to the same political party as the superintendent. He did as much as any other man, if not more, to secure his nomination for, and his election to, the office he now holds. For him to counsel the boy's expulsion from school or the infliction on him of any other punishment at all commensurate with his offence might so incense his father as to convert him from a warm and most valuable friend into a bitter and dangerous foe. "And," says the superintendent, " another election is near at hand, when I shall greatly need not only my friend's vote, but the votes of *his* numerous friends, first to carry the primaries and secure my renomination, and next to aid me at the polls on the day of election. The teacher is only a woman anyhow. She has no vote, and very few, if any, friends whose votes she can influence." Therefore he shirks a responsibility[1] which the duties of his office seemed to impose upon him, and throws it upon the shoulders of the school committee.

But when the school committee was appealed to we do not find that the matter was bettered in the least. And if the whole truth were known, it is not at all unlikely that they too had certain personal or political axes of their own to grind, and were also looking to the father of the offending boy for help.

But whatever may have been the particular *motive* of the school officials, the *fact* remains all the same that the teacher whom they had charged with the duty of maintaining the discipline of the school—just like thousands of other teachers similarly situated—found herself without the necessary authority, and utterly powerless to perform that duty. Not only that; she was compelled, in humiliation and shame, to pocket a most outrageous insult at the hands of an inferior, perpetrated in the presence of her whole school, and then had, moreover, to submit to be publicly snubbed by those whom the law had placed

---

[1] In the State referred to by Gail Hamilton the law slightly varies from that of California in its details but not in its principles.

above her, because she had dared to seek for relief in the only quarter where the law allowed her to seek it.

In order to realize how truly dependent, how pitiably humiliating is the position in which our boasted "*system*" places the teachers of its schools, it is only necessary to consider how perilous to their positions it would often prove for them to even attempt the enforcement of discipline amongst their pupils.

Open, as our common schools are, to all kinds of children, and the children of all kinds of parents, how rarely can it be truthfully said of one of these schools that there is not amongst its pupils even *one* who, if angered by its teacher, *could*, through its parents, exert sufficient influence over some one or more members of the school board to effect the teacher's removal?

And if even *one* such pupil be found in school, then will the teacher feel himself completely at its mercy.

But to be at the mercy of any *one* pupil in school is virtually to be at the mercy of *all*. For whenever it becomes known to the whole school that there is *one* of their number who can with impunity defy the teacher's authority, it will no longer be possible to find even *so many as one* who, in the light of such knowledge, will respect that authority.

We are fully aware that there are in our common schools many incompetent teachers, but we think we have now pretty clearly shown that the very *best* of teachers can not, as a rule, maintain discipline in these schools, and that for the double reason that the teacher has too little authority, and that this little comes from the wrong source, namely, from the *public* instead of the *parent*.

The failure of the pupil to make progress in his studies is almost sure to be attributed to the teacher's lack of ability to teach, whereas this failure not unfrequently results from the want of discipline.

It should be borne in mind that in a school where there is little or no discipline there can be little or no progress. It requires no argument to prove that even one unruly child, whom the teacher can neither govern nor expel, can so bedevil an entire school as to make study impossible. And without an application to study there *can* be no improvement.

The teacher, too, is generally made the scape-goat to bear the blame for all the demoralization and corruption of the school; whereas if St. Peter himself were the principal of one of these schools, with all the other apostles as assistant teachers; if he were compelled to receive into his school children of all kinds, classes, and characters, and of all degrees of moral depravity; if his authority over these children were not derived from their parents, but was only such as came from the political State; if he had not the privilege of making and enforcing rules for the government of his school, but were compelled to accept whatever rules and regulations *such* a board of politicians as the trickeries, the frauds, the briberies, and the accidents of an election might chance to place in power; and if, besides being denied the authority to either punish or expel, according to the dictates of his own judgment, refractory or corrupt and vicious pupils, he was furthermore forbidden to inculcate any principle of morality having for its object a higher aim than the gratification of man's animal appetites and earthly desires, we do not hesitate to declare it as our firm conviction, based on the foregoing reasons, that, as a rule, under such a system and subject to such degrading and humiliating conditions, not even St. Peter, with all the other apostles to help him, would find it possible, in the natural order of things, to check the swelling tide of common school immorality and crime. Except by rare chance, he could neither reform the least vicious nor shield from utter ruin the most virtuous children in his school.

If we are at fault in this conclusion, we are open to conviction, and shall take it as a favor if somebody will point out the fallacy of our reasoning. But if we are correct, then we ask, in all sincerity, if it is just and right to throw upon the *teachers* of our public schools *all* the blame for the lying and lechery, the dishonesty, impiety, and every other kind and degree of hopeless depravity which are to-day blasting and corrupting so many millions of our American common-school children? Every honest, intelligent, and capable common-school teacher *sees*, *feels*, and *laments* the evils of which we speak. It was a knowledge of these evils and of their parent causes which drew from the able and distinguished Dr. Joseph LeConte, a leading professor of our California State University, in the course of a letter to the writer of this article, the remark elsewhere quoted—

" That any education which weakens the family tie strikes at the very foundation of society, and no amount of good in other directions can atone for this greatest of evils."

It was this same knowledge which prompted the Hon. Ezra S. Carr, former State Superintendent of Public Instruction, in his official report for 1878–'79, page 39, when speaking of the workings of our common school system, to declare that—

" Dependence on one side and patronage on the other destroy the free and harmonious play of benefits between the home and the school;" and that

"*Private institutions, colleges, and seminaries draw away our best teachers, who thus avoid what is, to a sensitive and high-minded teacher,* an intolerable burden."

Similar to these also are the views of Gail Hamilton, a writer already quoted, who, at page 203 of her book, says:

" The tendency of our ' system ' is to degrade the teachers more and more by the, perhaps, unconscious subjection of the teacher's duties to the machinery."

On page 306 she adds:

" The ' system ' is constantly degrading teachers into menials, and concentrating authority in the hands of outside men who have nothing whatever to do with the actual teaching, and have the slightest possible contact with the children."

Now, we ask in all candor, if it is possible to degrade the teacher without degrading the pupil also? Can you degrade the master without degrading the disciple?

There is, there can be, no higher or more honorable occupation on this earth than that of a teacher who understands his calling and faithfully discharges its duties. Amongst all the poets, orators, sages, statesmen, and heroes of ancient Greece, where is there *one* whose illustrious name shines to-day with so bright and unfading a lustre as that of Socrates, the teacher of Athenian youth? And were we to blot out from the history of China the name and the teachings, and the fruits of the teachings, of Confucius, it would, so far as that country is concerned, be like blotting the sun from the heavens. The great mission of the Messiah Himself, on earth, was that of teacher.

Whatever country can boast of its great statesmen, great orators, great warriors, great jurists, great scientists, or of the great intelligence, morality, and virtue of its people, must acknowledge that, next to God, it is to its *teachers* it owes its highest debt of gratitude for so inestimable a boon.

But how is it possible for a teacher, though never so well qualified for his position, to earn this gratitude, who is not allowed to exercise his teaching qualifications?

Brought, as he is, in direct contact with, and required to govern, to teach, and to develop in due proportions all the faculties of a multitude of children, widely differing in mental powers, in moral training, in natural dispositions, in tastes, in physical constitutions, and in their modes of daily home life, there is probably no other calling which requires the exercise of more unrestrained freedom of action than does the calling of a principal or teacher of a school. And yet there is no other calling in which so little freedom is allowed in the performance of its duties.

Thus, for example, the physician who undertakes to doctor a patient reserves the liberty to prescribe both the kind and quantity of the medicines to be used, and the intervals at which they are to be taken, as well as the right to change his treatment whenever in *his* judgment such change is desirable. So, also, the mechanic who undertakes the job of building a good house always reserves the right both to choose his tools and to reject rotten or defective materials. But the common-school teacher can neither reject intractable nor rotten timber nor select the tools (the books) with which he is to do his work.

Not even the calling of a kitchen servant is near so dependent and servile as that of a common-school teacher under our present system, because even the kitchen servant has but *one* mistress to please in order to retain her place and earn her bread; whereas the common-school teacher, as we have seen, imperils his position every time he angers a child and incurs the displeasure of a parent who has influence with the school trustees.

Perhaps we may be asked, wherein consists the difference between the freedom or independence belonging to a private-school teacher and that which is enjoyed by the teacher of a public school?

We think that enough has already been said to render such difference quite apparent; but inasmuch as this is a very important branch of our subject, a few words more on that point may not be amiss.

In the first place, the man who proposes to establish a private school, just like a lawyer, a doctor, a merchant, a banker, or a mechanic, when seeking to build up a business, will rely chiefly upon his individual capacity and merit in order to secure employment. If he intends to make teaching his permanent business— and if not he had better go at something else—he will either buy, build, or rent his own school-house and premises, and procure his own school furniture. He will then establish his own rules and regulations, as well for the admission and expulsion of pupils as for their government and discipline while under his charge. These rules and regulations he will make known to those whose patronage he desires to secure, so that every parent or guardian who sends his children to such school will understand, at least in general terms, not only the rules by which they are to be governed, but also the character of the pupils with whom they are to associate. The teacher will also select for the use of his school the particular books by the use of which he believes himself capable of accomplishing the best results.

When parents send their children to such a school, it is because they agree with the teacher as to what sort of school is best for their children. In such a school there is no conflict or clashing between the jurisdiction of the parent and that of the teacher; because it is from the parents of each pupil, and only from its parents, that the teacher derives his authority to direct it, to teach it, to admonish it, to command it, and to enforce its obedience; and it is to the parents, and only to the parents of each, that he stands amenable for the manner in which he uses or abuses his powers. In such a school, so long as the teacher keeps within the scope of his authority, his counsels, his commands, and his chastisements become the counsels, the commands, and the chastisements of the child's own parents, because they come backed by parental authority and bearing the seal of the parental sanction. Should the pupil of a private school demand of his teacher by what authority he requires him to study this or that book, to refrain from this or that forbidden practice, to be present at a given hour, or to retire at the tap of a particular bell, the teacher need only reply—

" It is by the authority of your father, who loves you as he loves his own life. It was he, of his own free-will and choice—without reference to what others might think, say, or do—who placed you here. He selected this school because he himself had confidence in its teachers, approved of its rules, its discipline, and its course of study. Therefore you cannot violate the rules of the school, nor refuse obedience to its teachers, without disobeying your own father and mother, disobeying God, and proving yourself an unnatural, undutiful, and ungrateful child."

And what stronger motives—to discipline and study—than these could possibly be placed before the mind of an intelligent and well-bred youth?

But suppose that the *private* teacher, after having exhausted his authority in the way of counsel and correction, should still find his pupil refractory. What then? Why, he would dismiss or expel him of course. And if the father of the dismissed pupil should even have the wealth of the Vanderbilts, the Goulds, the Stanfords, and the Crockers combined, still he would not be able, even if so disposed, either to damage the school or to frighten the teacher out of one moment's peace of mind.

The noble independence of such a proceeding could but result in improving the discipline, strengthening the popularity, and swelling the ranks of the school. The expulsion of such a pupil could no more destroy the teacher's patronage than one of the Egyptian pyramids could be destroyed or overturned by plucking a single rotten pebble from its base and replacing it with a solid stone.

In cases of punishments not amounting to dismissal or expulsion, the most that *any* dissatisfied patron could do would be to withdraw his own children from school. But in all such cases let the teacher be sure to have right on his side, and for every pupil thus withdrawn he will gain two in its place. When a teacher has once succeeded in thus establishing a school of his own, resting on no other foundation than its merits, he is no more afraid of being turned out of his employment and left without the means of a support, because of having incurred the displeasure of one or a dozen discontented patrons of his school, than a lawyer, a doctor, or a merchant, when backed by the unbounded confidence of nearly an entire community, would be afraid of having his business ruined, and himself reduced to beggary, because of having incurred the enmity of a few unreasoning fault-finders.

Where, then, we would ask, is there a teacher to be found who would not to-day infinitely prefer the princely independence of teaching and managing a school under parental auspices, relying for patronage solely on his or her own merits—provided, of course, there are any merits to rely upon—rather than be compelled, as multitudes now are compelled, to beg, entreat. flatter, and fawn at the feet of pot-house politicians and public-school boards for the poor and pitiful privilege of playing the menial to their inferiors as the price of bread?

But here the inquiry presents itself: How would it be possible for all our public-school teachers, even if all were fully capable of teaching, to find a living patronage for schools under " parental auspices," so long as multitudes of parents would be unable to pay anything for their children's education, while other multitudes would be unwilling, after paying their school taxes into the public treasury, to pay, virtually, a second time for their children's education.

This, we confess, is, to a large extent, an insurmountable difficulty, so long as the present *anti-parental and teacher-enslaving* system remains intact. Although so odious is this system becoming in the eyes of thinking parents, as well as of intelligent teachers, that educational institutions established and run under private auspices are every day growing more and more into public favor. But for *this* fact, ex-Superintendent Carr would not have been able truthfully to declare, in the language already quoted, that—

" *Private institutions, colleges, and seminaries draw away our best teachers, who thus avoid what is to a sensitive and high-minded teacher an intolerable burden.*"

Yet it is only a comparatively limited number of parents who feel able to protect their children from the demoralizing and blighting effects of a State-school training, at so heavy a cost as the paying a second time for their education.

But, if it is true, as asserted by Prof. Joseph LeConte in his letter already quoted—

That "*private schools*, each parent choosing his own, furnish a better education, all things considered, that any public-school system;" and if it is *also* true, as maintained by ex-Superintendent Carr, that the public-school atmosphere is so much more uncongenial and unwholesome for "*high-minded teachers*" than is to be found in "*private* institutions;" in other words, if private institutions are so much better than the public ones, both for teachers and pupils, then we are confronted with this important question, namely:

Does not common sense suggest, and do not the true interests both of teachers and pupils demand, that the aforesaid schools of the *better* kind be multiplied, and those of the *inferior* kind diminished in numbers, in patronage, and in influence? And ought not this to be done as quickly and as rapidly as possible, until not a teacher in America, who is unwilling to be a slave for the pitiful consideration of a most precarious salary, and not a child, whose parents have so much as the least appreciation of the dignity or the responsibility of the parental office, shall any longer be victimized upon the altar of our false, servile, and ruinous system of education?

It seems clear to our mind that this question can only be answered in the affirmative, and that, therefore, the only remaining inquiry is, as to *how* so desirable a result can be accomplished.

As for ourselves we shall be satisfied with any just and practicable mode of accomplishing the end proposed. But until some other and better plan be suggested we shall still insist upon that which is outlined in the seventh proposition of our platform of principles. (See *ante* Chap. XIV.)

We are convinced that this, or some similar plan, by throwing open the whole business of teaching school to private enterprise and free competition, leaving every parent and guardian to select a school to suit himself, and requiring the State to pay for a good common secular education according to results in all cases where parents are unable to pay, would call to the front the very best and ablest teachers that the country affords. The adoption of such a plan would shatter the fetters that hold in bondage thousands of really good and competent teachers in our common schools, whose usefulness is now being destroyed, and the light of whose genius is being smothered beneath the accumulated rubbish of senseless rules and meaningless formalities.

Undoubtedly many of these teachers are capable of taking their places in the very front ranks of the world's greatest educational benefactors. And yet, after long years of labor, vexation, and disappointment, they find themselves neither understood nor appreciated, either in the public-school department or out of it. And the reason is that they are so circumscribed and hampered in their work that they have no more chance of displaying their real powers than an eagle would have to prove its ability to fly while kept in a cage with a baboon for a keeper.

There is, however, another class of public-school teachers who, like counterfeit coin, often pass for much more than their value. In fact, owing to a certain false and brassy glitter which they put on, they frequently outshine the pure gold of genuine worth.

But it is to the former class of public-school teachers that we now appeal for their countenance and support in aid of educational reform upon the plan just indicated.

Inasmuch as the establishment of this plan will result in forcing every teacher to rise or fall, to sink or swim, to survive or perish, according to his own individual merits or demerits, we know it would be vain for us to expect either aid, sympathy, or countenance from that other class of teachers who, being conscious of their own unfitness to teach a school, know full well that under the plan we propose *their* teaching career would be at an end.

To illustrate: Let us suppose that by the same cord we were to bind an eagle and a monkey to an inflated balloon; both would ascend with equal velocity, and both would rise equally high; but this would be a very poor test of their comparative powers of flight.

If, however, when in mid-air, it were proposed, in language intelligible to them both, to cut the cord which held them to the balloon, we think it would not be hard to tell, from the joyous and triumphant screams of the eagle compared with the pitiful shrieks and squalls of the monkey, which of the two could fly and which must fall.

Like unto this inflated balloon is our common - school system. Like unto an eagle tied to this balloon is many an able and highly-accomplished teacher, who could soar far higher without the system than with it; and like unto this monkey is many a worthless fraud, who rises and soars with the system, but who could neither rise nor soar without it.

Naturally enough, *these* are the implacable foes of the reform for which we plead. The others are at heart its friends.

The time has now arrived when it behooves these friends of genuine educational reform who hold positions in the public-school department to be up and doing. They *have* the power, if they will but *use* it, to do more for the advancement of this great cause than any other class of citizens, and in proportion to their power will be their responsibility. Their reputation, too, more than that of any other class, is involved in the issues here at stake.

It is every day becoming more and more apparent, from the inspection of statistics, that all over the country the growth of crime is commensurate with the spread, growth, and development of our common-school system.

To show that this growth of crime is going on within the temples of learning, and under the very eyes of our public - school teachers, we need only remind our readers of the statements repeatedly quoted by us, not only of leading public-school teachers of California, but also of Massachusetts, the boasted mother of the system.

For example: In the month of December, 1881, a California State Teachers' Institute was held in the city of San Francisco, and in the progress of its proceedings several of the leading teachers of our State schools made speeches, in the course of which, with scarcely a dissenting voice, it was declared that the children of our public schools were addicted to "*lying and dishonesty.*" (See reports of these speeches in the daily *Chronicle*, *Call*, and *Examiner* of December 28, 29, 1881; also see *Defender* of March, 1882.)

And we have on several occasions quoted the report, made by a committee of ladies, touching the result of their visits to the public schools of Massachusetts, for the purpose of ascertaining their moral condition, wherein they declared that—

"*The teachers almost universally complain of the prevalence of lying, stealing, profanity, and impurity among their scholars.*" (See *S. F. Chronicle*, October 3, 1880.)

Then, again, we have the statement, more general in its nature, quoted, as above, from the " Daily Public School," declaring that " *The most frequent failures* noticed in the reports are in the matter of *discipline or government.*"

And, of course, where there is " no discipline" or " government" there is no progress in knowledge, and no check upon vicious children or the growth of vice.

Now, the great and overshadowing question to which we desire to call the attention of the public-school teachers of America is this :

Where lies the chief blame for this want of discipline, and this consequent growth of demoralization and crime, in the public schools?

Is it true, as claimed by the author of the " Daily Public School," that the fault is in the *teachers?* Or is it true, as claimed by us, that the fault is in the *system* itself, by which the teachers are controlled?

And are we, or are we not, correct when we assert that, as a *general rule*, the very best teachers in the world, under this system, can have no satisfactory assurance of being able to preserve proper discipline or prevent the spread and growth of immorality and crime amongst their pupils?

Should any public-school teacher take the ground that the fault lies not in the " system " but in the teachers, we shall then ask him to tell us by what *practical* process, taking things as we find them, it would be possible, under our existing " *system*," to rid ourselves of the present *incompetent* teachers and to replace them with *better* ones.

But if, on the other hand, as we anticipate will be the case, every intelligent and really competent teacher will, on mature reflection, agree that the chief fault lies with our false system of education, then we shall earnestly ask, and confidently expect, the co-operation of *every such* teacher in our earnest efforts to sunder the shackles wherewith this " system " enslaves him, and binds down, in the dungeons both of ignorance and vice, millions of America's loveliest, brightest, and most gifted sons and daughters.

CHAPTER XVI.

COMPARISON BETWEEN THE PARENTAL AND ANTI-PARENTAL EDUCATIONAL SYSTEMS IN THE DEVELOPMENT OF GREAT MEN—DOES OPPOSITION TO ANTI-PARENTAL EDUCATION ARISE FROM BIGOTRY?

EXTRACT from a speech on the school question, delivered by the author before the Convention Committee on Education, at Sacramento City, November 20, 1878:

After two hundred years' trial, your Massachusetts State system produced annually, in proportion to her population, ten times as many native white criminals, nearly twice as many native white paupers, four times as many suicides of all classes, more than three times as many deaths from syphilis, and one and a half times as many insane persons as did the parental system of Virginia.

Then tell me what superior advantage Massachusetts has derived over Virginia from her anti-parental system of education. Is it found in the greater number and ability of her statesmen, in the superior eloquence of her orators, or in the greater courage, skill, and heroic achievements of her warriors?

It is undoubtedly true that Massachusetts has given to our country some of its very brightest and ablest literary men. The names of Prescott, Everett, and Bancroft—all students of Harvard University—and of William Cullen Bryant, who studied at Williams College, and of many other illustrious children of the old Bay State, are familiar as household words, and are pronounced with just pride wherever the English language is spoken; but it would be difficult to trace the literary greatness of one of these distinguished men to public-school training.

It is also true that Massachusetts gave birth to the illustrious Benjamin Franklin, but he was far more indebted for his education to his own mighty intellect, his indomitable perseverance, and the training of a Philadelphia printing office, than to the public schools of his native State. It is equally true that Massachusetts has given to the country two of its Presidents—the elder and the younger Adams. But it is no less true that they, too, were both educated at Harvard University, an institution which owes its origin rather to the private munificence of an Englishman than to the bounty of the State of Massachusetts. But as against these and a few lesser lights born upon the soil of Massachusetts, look at old Virginia's bright and glorious galaxy of statesmen, orators, and military heroes! Look at the long line of illustrious Presidents she has given to the Republic, beginning with the immortal Washington, the " Father of his Country," followed by Jefferson, Madison, Monroe, Harrison, Tyler, and the unconquerable old " Rough and Ready," the hero of Buena Vista. It was she who gave to our country the author of the world-renowned Declaration of American Independence. It was she who gave us that matchless orator, the incomparable Patrick

Henry, whose burning eloquence fired the American heart with the thrilling sentiments of that noble Declaration. To her belongs the honor of having given us the General-in-Chief to lead our half-famishing and half-naked armies triumphantly through the terrible and bloody war of the Revolution.

And when engaged in our more recent struggle with a neighboring republic, they were Virginia's chosen sons, Zachary Taylor and Winfield Scott, who carried our victorious arms in triumph into the very capital city of Mexico, and won for us this Golden State, whose destinies you, gentlemen, now hold in your hands. Then, again, when our late terrible civil war burst upon the country, there stood at the head of each opposing host a child of Old Virginia ; and throughout that fearful contest did the military prowess of the Old Dominion shine forth in all its pristine splendor.

However widely men may honestly differ as to the merits of that contest, there is no difference of opinion as to the manly courage, the splendid generalship, and the dauntless heroism of General Lee, of Stonewall Jackson, Turner Ashby, A. P. Hill, Joseph E. Johnston, and a host of other Confederate generals, whose earliest footprints were marked upon the soil of Old Virginia.

And against this mighty galaxy of generals whom Virginia gave to the Confederate cause, what did Massachusetts do for the other side? Why, she gave you the Union-sliding Banks and Benjamin F. Butler, which last was not her own child, by-the-by, but one who, like the great Daniel Webster, had been imported from the granite hills of New Hampshire.   * * *

Your humble servant has been sometimes charged with being a *bigoted Roman Catholic*, and with seeking to establish the public-school system on a sectarian basis. Now, that you may know how far my Catholic sectarianism carries me on this school question, allow me to assure you that, while I am an humble member of the Roman Catholic Church, and recognize to its fullest extent the teaching authority of that Church in religious matters, and, with a very few isolated exceptions, have the highest respect for the learning, ability, and piety of its clergy, yet if every priest and bishop in California and in America, backed by the Holy Father, the Pope of Rome himself, should do so improbable and unwarranted a thing as to command me to send my child to be educated by a particular teacher, whom I, as the father of the child, should conscientiously believe an unsuitable person to be entrusted with that important work, it would not only be my right, but my bounden duty, both as a *Roman Catholic and a parent*, to disobey the command ; and why? Because this a matter in which the law of nature throws upon me the responsibility of acting according to my own best judgment, based upon all the lights within my reach. Leaving all other considerations aside, is it at all probable that even all these priests, bishops, and Pope, with all their learning and piety, could know as much of the teacher's real character as I, the father, who daily read that character in the language and conduct of my own child?

And suppose that from that language and conduct, or from any

other source of information, I, the parent, should come to the conclusion that the teacher of my young son or daughter is an unprincipled libertine, whose detestable conduct or vile maxims would,
in a single day, or, perhaps, in a single moment, corrupt and ruin
my child—shall it be said that I must still wait until my priest or
bishop, or any other man, whether he be churchman or statesman,
shall grant me permission to snatch my child from the jaws of destruction?

No! no! This is a power, an authority over my child, which,
whilst living, I can neither entrust to nor divide with any other man.[1]

And the very same right which I claim for myself I claim for every
other parent, be he Catholic, Protestant, Jew, or non-religionist;
and this is the length, the breadth, the height, the depth, and the
thickness of my Roman Catholic sectarianism on the school question; and when I speak thus I believe I speak the sentiments of
every well instructed Roman Catholic in the world, except it be a
certain nondescript kind usually styling themselves Liberal Catholics, and whom, in California, you may generally know by the fact
that, whenever in their presence the charge of religious bigotry is
preferred against your humble servant in connection with this school
question, they always stand ready to shout *Amen!* to the slander.

This is a class of Catholics, every one of whom, while agreeing
with me that it would be wrong to surrender his parental authority
to any bishop or priest, no matter how learned and holy he might
be, would not at the same time hesitate to divide that authority with
every hoodlum and loafer and bummer and drunkard; with every
thief, rake, and robber, provided only they have votes with which to

---

[1] The question may perhaps be asked: Does not the Roman Catholic Church to-day command its members to withhold their children
from anti-parental and Godless public schools? And do not Catholic parents consider themselves in conscience bound to obey the
command? We answer most assuredly, Yes! And if that Church
should command its members to keep their children out of the fire,
every intelligent and conscientious Catholic parent would doubtless
feel bound to obey *that* command also. But suppose a priest or
bishop or Pope, or all these combined, not only in violation of the
command of their Church, but in defiance of the plainest dictates
of the natural law, should order a Catholic parent to cast his
children *into* the fire, would it logically follow from the foregoing proposition that he must obey such an order as this? On
the contrary, the moral law being incorporated into the Catholic's
creed, and forming, as it does, an essential part thereof, no Catholic,
who has been sufficiently educated in his religion to know what the
moral law is, can ever regard it as a conscientious duty to violate
that law in obedience to the dictates of any mortal man. Hence we
do not hesitate to assert that if the Pope himself should command a
Catholic parent, or any other parent, to send his children to an anti-
parental, Godless, and crime-producing school, against his own
judgment and conscience, it would be his duty *not* to obey.

lift his miserable carcass into some petty office, where, with the prefix of honorable to his name, he will seek to cover his worse than Judas-like treason—treason to his children, treason to his country, and treason to his God.

It has not unfrequently been said to me: "Were it not for your radical and uncompromising notions on the school question you could have this office, and that office, and the other office." I now give due notice, both to my friends and my foes, that I recognize no more honorable office on earth than the office of vindicating down-trodden truth, and I may add that I neither ask nor desire any higher office than the office of stripping and exposing in all their horrid and naked deformity, and lashing with the relentless scourge of truth, these trimming, time-serving, pot-house politicians, whether of high or low degree, called *Liberal Catholics*, who would not only barter their own birthright, but that of their children, and their children's children, to the end of time for a dirty mess of political pottage.

CHAPTER XVII.

MR. HENRY GEORGE AND REV. DR. MCGLYNN ON THE SAME PLATFORM.

In the New York *Freeman's Journal* of July 15, 1882, was copied from the *New York Sun* a synopsis of a speech delivered by Rev. Dr. McGlynn, of St. Stephen's Church, on the occasion of the then recent Davitt reception, which runs as follows:

The Rev. Dr. McGlynn, of St. Stephen's Church, took the stand after Mr. Swinton   Dr. McGlynn addressed the throng as " Ladies and Gentlemen," adding that he presumed that there must be working-women among them. He was glad to join in bidding Godspeed to Michael Davitt. He would make no apologies for being there, in spite of the length of his coat and his sacerdotal countenance. If anybody asked what the priest was doing there, anyhow, he would say that, being a priest, he did not lose his character as a man. [Applause.]   A good priest ought to be a good man, and a great man.   [Applause.]   No cause could be worthy of the applause and sacrifices of men unless it was the cause of universal man. He was not ashamed to say he did not set up for a bloated aristocrat; and he would say, as there were enough there to keep the secret, that he was not much of a lover of bloated aristocrats. The fact that he was a priest was an additional reason why he should be there. The cause of suffering, martyred poor in Ireland was the cause of true religion. If there seemed to be a divorce between the Church and the masses, it was not the fault of the masses. Perhaps it would be better for the clergy to come a little oftener out of their pulpits and come a little nearer to the people to discover the cause of their complaint, and, if possible, to apply the remedy. [Applause long continued.]   Christ himself was but an evicted peasant.

He had complained that, though the foxes had holes, and the birds of the air nests, the Son of Man had not where to lay His head. Christ had come to teach the poorest man that He was all of a man, and the taskmaker that he, too, was only a man, bound to the duties of common humanity.

As to the land question, he would say, first, that the commandment that bore upon that question was, " Thou shalt not steal." But who was it that was doing the stealing? The landlords would say : " Do not dare to touch the pig that pays the rent." It would be a calamity if anything should befall the gentleman that pays the rent. [Laughter.] The poor people of Ireland had got to believe that they must pay the rent, even if, after they had paid rent, they had to lie down and starve. But they had now come to believe that they might eat the pig themselves and throw the feet to the landlords. [Laughter.] The teachings of Davitt and Parnell were rapidly bringing the people to a knowledge of their rights. Was it possible that God could see without displeasure the state of affairs in Ireland? Such was not God's will, and men were not forbidden to curse such a system of iniquity. He claimed the right of human beings on this earth to so live that they might prepare themselves for a life hereafter. He asked the blessing of God on Michael Davitt and such as he who were fighting the battle of the people. He would not have Mr. Davitt explain his gospel, but to preach it. We might have the same problem to solve in this country, and the sooner we solve it the better. He stood on the same platform as Henry George and Bishop Nulty, of Meath. [Applause.] If he did not feel that he was standing on the eternal platform of eternal truth, liberty, and justice, he would not stand on that platform. As a Christian minister, he invoked the blessing of God upon Michael Davitt. The truth needed martyrs like him.

The Rev. Dr. McGlynn said that the more Irishmen the British Government put in jail the more effectual would the Irish movement become. Ireland would never gain anything from a sense of justice in the British Parliament. The only way was to excite British fears. The Englishman's heart was in his pocket, and if you attacked his pocket you attacked him in his most vital point. Dr. McGlynn had cordially approved of the " no-rent" manifesto from the beginning. The landlords never owned the lands, and, therefore, no rent could be due them. The non-payment of rent was justifiable on military principles. When a country was in a state of war or siege it was right to refuse supplies to the enemy. Ireland had been petitioning for centuries for the eighth of a loaf to eat, and had been turned away by the British Parliament. He advised Ireland to take the half loaf that was now offered by Parliament, and after that had been digested to sing out for the other half.

While there are some things contained in the above synopsis of Rev. Dr. McGlynn's remarks which will challenge the approval of every friend of poor, down-trodden, and long-suffering Ireland, there are, at the same time, other things which we cannot read without alarm, especially when we remember that they come as the utterances of a talented, eloquent, and influential priest of the Roman Catholic Church. Among other things, the reverend speaker is represented as declaring that " *he stood on the same platform as Henry George and Bishop Nulty, of Meath.*"

Now, while there seems to be some differences of opinion as to the precise position occupied on the land question by the Bishop of Meath, there can be no doubt as to that of Mr. Henry George, unless he has changed ground quite recently. In his work entitled " Progress and Poverty," published about two years ago, he most, clearly, explicitly, and with great force and ability announced his sentiments on the land question. And if the views and sentiments of Mr. Henry George, as set forth in this work, constitute his platform, and the same platform is endorsed by Rev. Dr. McGlynn, then we have only to read Mr. George's said work in order to learn Rev. Dr. McGlynn's position. Mr. George, in the volume referred to, boldly proclaims the doctrine that private property in land is unjust, and the five chapters of the seventh book of his work, as above entitled, are devoted to the task of maintaining this proposition. As a sample of the ultra-communistic doctrines set forth in Mr. George's platform, as expressed in his work, we here quote from page 305, where he says: "Though the sovereign people of the State of New York consent to the landed possessions of the Astors, the puniest infant that comes wailing into the world in the squalidest room of the most miserable tenement house becomes at that moment seized of an equal right with the millionaires. And it is robbed if the right is denied." In a foot note on the same page Mr. George calls this " a natural and inalienable right to the equal use and enjoyment of land." By way of supporting so startling a theory the author asks what it is that " constitutes the rightful basis of property? What is it that enables a man to justly say of a thing, 'It is mine?' From what springs the sentiment which acknowledges his exclusive right as against all the world? Is it not, primarily, the right of a man to himself, to the use of his own powers, to the enjoyment of the fruits of his own exertions? Is it not this individual right which springs from, and is testified to by, the natural facts of individual organization— the fact that each particular pair of hands obey a particular brain and are related to a particular stomach; the fact that each man is a definite, coherent, independent whole—which alone justifies individual owership? As a man belongs to himself, so his labor, when put in a concrete form, belongs to him." For this reason, says Mr. George: "That which a man makes or produces is his own, as against all the world, to enjoy or to destroy, to use, to exchange, or to give. * * * * The pen with which I am writing is justly mine. No other being can rightfully lay claim to it, for in me is the title of the producers who made it. It has become mine, because transferred to me by the importer, who obtained the exclusive right to it by transfer from the manufacturer, in whom, by the same process of purchase, vested the rights of those who dug the material from the ground and shaped it into a pen. Thus my exclusive right of ownership in the pen springs from the natural right of the individual to the use of his own faculties."

We propose now to examine briefly the foundation whereon Mr. George rests his theory that there cannot justly be any private property in land; and we shall undertake the task of showing that in order to be logical, and to maintain a position in harmony with the fundamental proposition whereon rests his whole theory, it will be necessary to go still farther and deny that there is or can be any such thing as a title to private property vested in man, whether such property be land or anything else.

As we have just seen, Mr. George, as the basis of all property rights in man, asserts the proposition that "*man belongs to himself,*" and that "therefore what he makes or produces," and only what he makes or produces, "is his own, as against all the world, to enjoy or destroy, to use, to exchange, or to give."

Now, it seems to us scarcely possible for any other writer to crowd so great a number of such gigantic fallacies into the same space as are contained in the foregoing propositions. In the first place we deny that "man belongs to himself," and in order to make good our denial it is only necessary to invoke another proposition advanced by the same learned author. For example: On the very page where this self-ownership of man is so triumphantly asserted, it is further maintained that, because of man's ownership of himself, whatever he "makes or produces is his own." If, then, it is true that the making of a thing gives the maker title to the thing made, man unquestionably belongs, *not to himself*—unless it can be shown that he made himself—but to God, his creator. And upon this palpably false proposition rests Mr. George's whole theory. But even if this false proposition were true, and if it were admitted that man really owns himself, still, according to Mr. George's idea as to the mode, and the only mode, of acquiring title to property, such acquisition would be utterly impossible, for, as we have just seen, the only original mode of acquiring title to property, according to Mr. George, is to make or produce it.   Now to make a thing, in its true and proper sense, means to create it.   But man can create nothing.   Not so much as one grain of sand.   No, nor even so much as the very smallest invisible mote or atom of matter. But our author would say : " When I used the word ' *make* ' I did not exactly mean to *create*, hence I coupled with it the word ' *produce*,' " meaning, thereby, simply changing the form of some material substance.   Such a change, for example, as the farmer brings about when he is instrumental in converting the earth's rich soil into corn, beans, and potatoes, or the lumberman and the mechanic when they fell the forest trees and convert them into houses, or the brick manufacturer when he works sand and clay into mortar and moulds them into brick.   This, we presume, is the sense in which Mr. George intends to be understood when he uses the words " *make or produce*."

But here again the learned author's logic murders itself.   On page 302 he maintains that " no one can be rightfully entitled to the ownership of anything which is not the produce of his labor, or the labor of some one else from whom the right has passed to him."   And upon this ground he over and over again insists that there cannot justly be any such thing as private property in land, because no man can make or produce land.   Now, who does not know that every tree and herb, every grain of corn, and every blade of grass that grows ; every beast, every bird, and every insect is formed from, and, in fact, constitutes a part of the very substance and cream of the land?   Now, if a man cannot *make land*, neither can he make that particular and most valuable ingredient in the land, which enters into the growth and forms, as we have just said, the very substance both of animal and vegetable matter.   And if man does not and cannot own the land, of which these things are made, how is it possible for him to own the things themselves?   Should a thief take a bar of silver to which he had no title, but which belonged to another, and melt and run it into coin or silver spoons, no honest judge in the world would say that the mere fact of his having expended his skill and labor upon this piece of stolen metal could possibly give him a title either to the coin or the spoons into which he had manufactured it.   Neither does it seem any more possible to change the rightful ownership of the soil by converting it into porridge than it does to change the ownership of a silver bar by converting it into spoons with which to eat the porridge.   According to Mr. George's theory, if we understand it aright, the man who, with his hard and honestly earned money, purchases a field from one who holds a title, recognized as genuine by the solemn sanctions of his country's laws and the general consent of mankind, is, nevertheless, a robber if he denies that " *the puniest infant that comes wailing into the world in the squalidest room of the most miserable tenement house becomes at that moment seized of an equal right* " with himself. Nor do the monstrous conclusions of this strange logic even stop here. For, according to Mr. George, while the man who, under the solemn sanctions of law and with the general consent of mankind, invests his money in the purchase of land is a *robber* if he claims anything by virtue of his purchase, his neighbor, on the other hand, who neither invested a cent in said land nor inherited it from any one who has, and who, against the protest of the purchaser, in violation of the statutes of his country, and in defiance of the common judgment of mankind, would, by intrusion, take joint possession with such purchaser, and without consideration appropriate to his own use the soil which had been so purchased and enriched by another, would for so doing be worthy of all commendation as an honest and upright man! Truly, if this is not the robber's gospel we know not what is.

It seems to us that Mr. George's false conclusions as to what he calls the " injustice of private property in land " are at least partly due to his erroneous ideas as to what really constitutes the highest human title to property and the exact nature and extent of such title. The kind or degree of title of which he seems to be speaking rests, as we have seen, upon the false assumption that man is the absolute owner of himself, and, consequently, that he is the absolute owner of whatever he makes or produces, (although he make it out of God Almighty's material), and that the character of this owner-ship is such as gives him the right, not only to use and enjoy as he pleases, but even to utterly destroy the thing owned. Such a title as *this* we hold none but God alone possesses, because it is not *man*, as claimed by Mr. George, but only God who owns himself; and, consequently, it is only God who can rightfully claim the absolute and ultimate title to himself and to the things he has made, no difference whether those things be in the shape of lands, or cattle, or of fruits, flowers, and fields of waving grain. Neither do we see how it is possible for either Mr. George or his reverend follower to escape these conclusions without either denying the existence of God, who made all things, or else repudiating his own premises wherein it is asserted as a fundamental proposition that he, and *only* he, who owns himself owns also that which he has made.

If a man belongs absolutely to himself, then he is responsible only to himself for his dealings with himself; and whether, on the one hand, he live the life of a lazy, worthless sot, and die the horrible death of the suicide, or whether, on the other, he lead a sober, industrious, virtuous life, and then die a natural and honorable death— in either case he will have but exercised what Mr. George would call his inalienable right to do as he pleases with that which belongs to himself.

This brings us to a point where it will be in order to define what we understand to be the nature and extent of man's ownership in property, whether it be in the nature of lands or of goods and chattels.

In order to have a clear idea of the nature and limits of man's title to property we must constantly bear in mind the fact, as already suggested, that man did *not* make himself, but that he was made by another, and, consequently, that he does *not* belong to himself, but that he belongs to another. That his entire physical, mental, and moral self; his body, with its flesh and blood, and bone and marrow; its every muscle, fibre, and atom of matter, from the very tip of his hair to the end of his little toe-nail; his soul, with its will, memory, and understanding; and, in fact, every faculty which it is possible for him to use, either in the acquisition of knowledge or the accumulation of worldly wealth, are all the absolute property of his Creator. That the earth, the air, and the ocean, with all their teeming wealth of animate and inanimate things, are also the **property** of Him who created them. Therefore whatever title man has acquired, or can acquire, to any species of property, whether it be land or personal chattels, must of necessity be from God, the only true owner, and subject at all times to His supreme will and control. That man has a genuine but subordinate title to the earth and the ocean, with all their varied productions, is manifest not only from the testimony of natural reason, but also from the words of holy writ, for in the first chapter of Genesis it is written that God said : " Let us make man to our own image and likeness ; and let him have dominion over the fishes of the sea, and the fowls of the air, and the beasts, and the whole earth, and every creeping creature that moveth upon the earth." Here, then, is the source of man's title, not only to his personal goods and chattels, but to his landed estates as well. For it will be observed from the language just quoted that man's " dominion " was not to be limited to the " fishes of the sea, and the fowls of the air, and the beasts," but was to be extended to " *the whole earth*," as well as to " every creeping thing that moveth upon the earth " Here, then, is man's title-deed, through which he traces back to his Lord and Maker his right to property, both *real* and *personal*.

It may be that Mr. George denies the genuineness of our title-deed, but we presume the reverend New York convert to Mr. George's platform, with whom we are partly dealing, will not join in that denial.

We have said that man's title to property, both real and personal, is but a subordinate and qualified one, subject at all times to the superior and ultimate title of the Creator, and of this fact we must not lose sight. In order that we may the more certainly keep this fact steadily in view, let us inquire a little more closely into the reason for this limitation upon man's title to property. No intelligent being has ever yet knowingly and designedly put into shape anything without a purpose. And the Almighty, being infinitely wise, has neither made nor done anything without an infinitely *wise* purpose. And being infinitely good, He has neither made nor done anything without an infinitely *good* purpose. Hence we are led to conclude that when He made the earth, the air, and the ocean, with all their elements of material wealth, He must have made them for an infinitely wise and an infinitely good purpose. Consequently, when He gave to man dominion over all these things it must have been His will that he use them in a manner to correspond with the objects for which they were made. But what was the Almighty's object in creating these elements of worldly wealth of which we are speaking? Was it not to promote His own honor and glory, and at the same time to supply man's proper physical, mental, and moral wants, and thereby to contribute to his happiness?

The gift by the Almighty to man of dominion over the earthly creation was of course a gift in common, whereby every human being was allowed to draw from this common and abundant heritage, and appropriate to his own use such articles—not previously appropriated—as were suited to his necessities, tastes, and lawful desires. And when men began this process of individual appropriation, then and there began the origin and history of private property, without the necessity of man's having to *make* an article as the only test of his rightful ownership. The man who first found a wild turkey's nest, a swarm of bees, or a precious stone upon unclaimed land, did not *make* either the bees, the turkey eggs, or the precious stone; and yet, if he chose to have it so, they became his property by the mere act of appropriation. If the learned author of " Progress and Poverty " were to go into a wild forest, and cut the timber and saw the lumber with which to build him a house, he would doubtless say that the house, when built, was *his*, because he *made* it.   But was not the *material his* even before he built the house?   And yet he did not make the material.   If, after he had selected his lumber tree, and was on the ground ready for work, clearly indicating his purpose—even before his axe had pierced the outer bark—some later claimant had made his appearance and objected to his cutting the tree, would he not have said, " Sir, this is my tree !"   But according to Mr. George's theory, by what right could he have claimed that it was his tree?   For surely he had not made the tree, any more than he had made the land whereon the tree had grown.   Hence, we claim that Mr. George is in error when he assumes that it is impossible for man justly to have private property in a thing which was not *made* or produced either by himself or by some other person, viz., some other human being, whose title he holds.   And it is upon this erroneous assumption that our author denies the justice of private property in land ; that is to say, because man did not make the land.   But if it is true that, by the simple act of appropriation, man can become the rightful owner of a nest of turkey eggs, a swarm of bees, a precious stone, or a timber tree, which neither he nor any human being whose title he claims ever made or produced, then upon what principle can it be said that, by a similar act of appropriation, man *cannot* justly acquire private property in land not previously appropriated?

It must be borne in mind, however, that man's title to property, whether in land or in movables, and whether held in community or in severalty, is a *qualified and limited* title in the nature of a *trust,* coupled with an obligation to so use such property as to subserve the end for which it was created, namely : the honor of God and the welfare of man.   Therefore, it is not true, as held by Mr. George, that man holds, or can hold, even what he calls his own property, by such an absolute title as to give him *ipso facto* a right to destroy that property.   To show, by a simple illustration, how monstrous is the doctrine here asserted by our author, let us suppose the case of a very wealthy man, who counts his money by the millions of dollars.   He neither owns nor claims to own a foot of land, and his money has all come to him through what Mr. George would call just and legitimate channels.   To make the matter clear, we will suppose that he has dug every dollar of it with his own pick and shovel out of the rich placers of California.   No sooner has he amassed this immense fortune than he learns that a most deadly plague has simultaneously attacked the people of New York, Boston, Philadelphia, Charleston, Savannah, Baltimore, Cincinnati, St.

Louis, Chicago, Louisville, New Orleans, and San Francisco, and is rapidly spreading to all the neighboring towns and cities, and even into the homes of the rural districts. He has further learned that *one* and *only one* remedy has been found for this dreadful destroyer of his race, and that remedy is quinine. With the quickness of thought a gigantic project is resolved upon, and in the execution of this project he immediately telegraphs to every druggist in the United States, purchasing, at whatever cost, all the quinine in the country. This quinine he causes to be shipped to New York, and there securely stored in an iron warehouse. Owing to this complete monopoly of the only medicine that could cure the plague, death is mowing down men, women, and children by tens and even hundreds of thousands per day. By the use of quinine every patient could be cured; without it not one can live. Our millionaire is besieged with applications for the precious drug. But all to no purpose. First one thousand, then five, then ten thousand dollars per ounce are proffered. And while the wealthy ply him with offers of money, the poor, in the name of God and humanity, beseech and implore, on bended knees and with tearful eyes, for just enough medicine to save a perishing daughter, a stricken son, a dying wife, or an expiring mother. But no! Neither for the love of money nor in the name of sweet charity will he let go so much as one solitary atom of his hoarded medicine, and, finally, in the exercise of what Mr. George claims to be his undoubted right (to either " enjoy or destroy" his own property) he causes this entire stock to be dumped into the ocean, leaving millions of his countrymen to perish who could and would have been saved if such a wretch as he had never been born. Yet, according to the ethics of Mr. Henry George's platform, this diabolical act of wholesale murder would be but the exercise of a man's right to do as he pleases with his own property. As for ourselves, we plead guilty to such a degree of obtuseness in our moral vision that we cannot possibly distinguish the difference between the guilt of the monster who would expend his money in the purchase of poison for the wanton destruction of human life and that other monster who, when the fatal poison of a raging pestilence was doing its work of death, would use *his* money for the purchase and destruction of the only antidote which could save the lives of the infected.

Or, take another illustration: If a man has a right to do as he pleases with the property which Mr. George would call his own, because his labor has earned it, then who can censure the drunken husband and father who, on every Saturday night, squanders his week's wages for whiskey, while the wife of his bosom and the children of his loins are left naked and hungry, to shiver with cold and to die of starvation? And if this theory of Mr. George's, which holds that the lawful owners of personal property have a right to do with it as they please, is a true one, it furnishes a complete justification for all the outrages that were ever practised upon poor suffering humanity by any and every species of monopolists— except land monopolists—from the morning of creation down to the present moment, provided, only, that such monopolists acquired their wealth either by producing it or else by securing to themselves the title of the producers. According to this doctrine, the man of money may buy up all the food within a thousand miles of his plethoric store-houses, and thus force provisions up to starvation prices, spreading famine, starvation, and death amongst the poor, and yet do nothing but what a man may rightfully do with his own property.

The solemn truth is that man does not, never did, and never can, own property in that absolute sense in which Mr. George seems to understand the word " *ownership.*" It is only the Almighty, we repeat, who does or can own property in that absolute sense ; and when He entrusted man with dominion over *His* property He never authorized him to use it for any purpose antagonistic to the great object for which he created it. When Dives refused to allow poor Lazarus to eat the crumbs that fell from his table he did exactly what Mr. George claims he had a right to do, because these were the crumbs of Dives, and Mr. George says a man has a right to do as he pleases with his own property. And yet, because Dives, like our New York divine, chose to stand upon Mr. Henry George's platform, the Scripture assures us that when he *died* he was buried in hell.

No, it is not true that man has a right to use even the productions of his own hands as he pleases, unless he should please to use them in accordance with the great law of justice and charity ; in other words, unless he please to use them for the honor and the glory of the Almighty Giver and the good of man—for man simply holds property in trust, and it is only thus that he can execute that trust. It is true that along with this trust comes the right to the personal use of so much of the trust-fund as is proper to gratify the possessor's lawful desires and to contribute to his individual legitimate comfort, as well as the comfort of those depending upon him, but the " crumbs " that fall from his table, namely, wealth not needed for other purposes, should not be withheld from the hungry, the naked, and the homeless. He is the Almighty's almoner, and is, therefore, morally a criminal if he wastes his Master's substance and leaves the poor to perish.

We do not say that the rich man should recklessly distribute all his surplus wealth indiscriminately amongst his needy neighbors, leaving himself no surplus capital with which to accumulate more. Not at all ; for this would be like turning a lot of thoughtless, hungry children into the buttery, where they would soon eat themselves sick and waste more than they would eat. But the truly charitable man should not fail to hold the reins of prudence over his liberality. We hold that every man has, primarily, a moral right to the free use and enjoyment of so much property as he can honestly acquire, either by appropriation, by labor, by inheritance, by purchase, or by exchange, whether in lands or personal chattels.

When we speak of honestly acquiring property, we mean acquiring it in such manner as does not interfere with the vested rights of others.

Enough has already been said to show that he who would overturn all human title to land, upon the ground that man did not *make* the land, need not be long in finding an equally plausible reason for denying likewise all title to personal property. Because, as already remarked, man did not make the *material* which enters into and constitutes the very substance of all kinds of personal property. And if, as claimed by Mr. George, the man who, with the highest sanction of human law, enters upon and appropriates to himself a piece of hitherto unappropriated land, clears the dense forests, cuts away the roots, plows the ground, plants him an orchard, builds him a house, and digs him a well, acquires no title to the land because he did not make it, then may it not, with at least equal justice, be contended that the man who, under the sanction of the same human law, digs down into the bowels of the earth and draws forth coal or iron, or copper or silver, or gold or precious stones, has no title and can convey no title to any of these things, because, forsooth, he did not make them ? And would not the same kind of logic serve equally well to prove an industrious, thrifty farmer to be a heartless robber, who would deny to his indolent neighbors an equal right with himself to take and eat the corn from his crib and the bacon from his meat-house, because these articles of food were drawn from and are, in fact, a part of the substance of the land ?

We are fully aware that Mr. George does not yet carry his doctrines to the extent of denying the justice of man's title to *personal* property, but what we maintain is, that the logic of these doctrines, if followed to its legitimate conclusion, would of necessity lead to that result. Let Mr. George's premises be generally accepted and it will not be long before some more logical communist than he, building upon the foundation which he has laid, will readily reach the climax just indicated.

Mr. George's communistic theories would be far less dangerous in this country were it not for the fact that so much has been and is daily being done by the American people to prepare the public mind for their favorable and logical acceptance. When the doctrine is boldly proclaimed that every child born into the world may demand, not simply as a charity due to the poor, but as a right due to all, that he be educated at the public expense, there can be no logical denial of the fact that the general acceptance of such a doctrine is the practical acceptance of a communism even broader and more sweeping in its grasp than that contended for by the author of "Progress and Poverty."

If, as maintained by Blackstone, and Kent, and Wayland, and every other standard author on either law or morals, it is the natural duty of parents to "feed, to clothe, and to educate" their own children; in other words, if parents are under the very same obligation to supply their own children with a proper education that they are to supply them with proper victuals and clothes, is it not just as communistic to take one man's money with which to educate the children of another, when that other is in duty bound to educate them himself, as it would be to take the same man's money with which to feed and clothe the same children?

"Communism," as defined by Webster, means "the doctrine of a community of property, or the negation of individual rights in property." Now, if the man who has earned, or otherwise lawfully acquired, property has no individual right thereto as against his neighbors who desire to use it for the education of *their* children, why may not these same neighbors with equal justice declare that he has no individual right to the same property against those who choose to take it for the feeding and clothing of their children? And if they may rightfully communize—so to speak—his property for the feeding and clothing of their children, why may they not with like justice "communize" the same property for the feeding and clothing of themselves? In fact, if it is just and right to force the whole people to put their private property into a common fund in order to supply the educational wants of children which the natural law requires their fathers and mothers to supply at their individual expense, we can see no logical reason why the whole people might not justly and rightfully be forced to put their individual property into a like common fund in order to supply any other want which the natural law requires each member of society to supply for himself. We are not now denying the propriety or the justice of levying a tax to pay, to a certain extent, for the education of children whose parents are unable to educate them. That is undoubtedly justifiable upon the same grounds upon which we would justify the furnishing of both children and parents with victuals and clothes at public expense whenever their necessities were such as to render them objects of public charity. But the levy of a public-school tax for the education of all the children in the State, rich as well as poor, rests upon no such foundation. The levy of this communistic public-school tax for the maintenance of schools instituted for all the children is, by the advocates of the system, sometimes likened to the levy of a public-road tax, or a tax for the support of the Government. But the cases are by no means parallel, as a moment's reflection will show. To construct or to take care of a public road is in no proper sense a private duty. If it were, we could no more rightfully shift that private duty on to the public shoulders than any other private duty. If the road to be built or repaired, instead of being a public road, were a private one within the proprietor's own enclosure, where is there an honest man whose sense of justice would not revolt at the idea of taxing the public to pay for the construction or repair of such a road? As for the man whose domestic relations are of so unsatisfactory a character that he is unable to claim any individual rights in the children which he calls his, other than such as he may properly accord to his neighbors, we can see no injustice in his demanding that those neighbors assist him in supplying such children with the means of an education. But whoever, when looking upon a child of his household with the faith and confidence of one who has never for a moment distrusted the fidelity of its mother, can say with unfaltering faith, " This, indeed, is *my child !*' ought never, never, to repudiate the high, the holy, and the God-imposed obligation of educating such child. Indeed, according to our humble way of thinking, there is no kind or degree of communism so utterly revolting as that which, for educational purposes, virtually asserts a community of title, not only to the property, but also to the children of the private citizen. Yet, this, unfortunately, is the communism of America ; a communism having for its main trunk an educational system the most ruinously expensive and the most demoralizing that the world ever saw. A communism whose poisonous roots have spread far and wide, and struck deep down into the soil of American literature, American politics, and, we may say, American religion.

Millions of American children, of all creeds, classes, and conditions, daily gather beneath the wide-spreading branches and inhale the poisonous odors of this deadly upas. Tens of thousands of these little ones die annually from diseases contracted in its overcrowded and tainted atmosphere, while hundreds of thousands meet a moral death ten thousand times worse for themselves, their parents, and their country than that physical death which consigns its victims to an untimely grave. These children, as a rule, grow to manhood and womanhood without any proper knowledge of the duties which they owe to their fathers and mothers, to their country or their God. About the only thing which they are taught touching the rights of property is, that every child born into the world is entitled to an education at the expense of the community, which, as we have seen, is the very quintessence of the logic of communism. Under these circumstances, with the whole educating power of the country enlisted in the work of inculcating into the minds of American youth both the doctrines and practices of communism, and the whole political power of both State and Federal Governments backing the movement, how long will it be before the morally depraved and penniless portion of Young America, with the sword in one hand and the torch in the other, will demand of the wealthy an equal share of their worldly goods, and, in the language of Mr. George, will call it " robbery " if their demand be denied?

And when this anti-parental, Godless, and communistic training, which so many millions of American children are now receiving, shall have matured its legitimate fruits of violence and blood and plunder, whither shall the guilty authors and architects of ruin—the uncompromising friends and advocates of this kind of training—find protection, either for their liberty, their lives, or their material wealth? Will they invoke the shield of the law? Alas! they will find, to their bitter sorrow, that those whom they have taught to despise parental authority, and to ignore both God and His commandments, will respect no law but that of their own unbridled appetites. Will they rely for protection upon physical force? Unfortunately for them the physical force will be upon the other side. When, therefore, the evil day shall come, let not the man of means—who now boastfully pours out his money like water in order to indoctrinate the rising generation in the false and dangerous principles of communism—shrink from the logical results of his own blind folly. To-day he sows the wind ; to-morrow let him prepare to reap the whirlwind.

Mr. Henry George draws a frightful and, undoubtedly in the

main, a very truthful picture of the poverty, misery, and degradation which have been, and are being, brought about by the improper use of large fortunes, whereby the poor are daily becoming poorer and the rich richer.   This, however, is not the necessary result of accumulated wealth, but arises, first, from the dishonest and even diabolical means resorted to for its procurement ; and next, from the mean, sordid, selfish, and criminal uses for which it is employed by those who hold with Mr. George that they have a right to do as they please with their own property.

Great worldly wealth, whether in land or money, just like great worldly learning, like steam, electricity, and the printing-press, is a great power either for good or evil, depending mainly for its good or bad fruits upon the good or bad purposes for which it is used, and the purposes for which it is used depend chiefly upon the good or bad qualities of the man by whom it is used.   For the bad use and the consequent evil results to society from each and all of these mighty engines of power, whether they be in the shape of worldly wealth, worldly wisdom, or anything else, we know of but one effectual remedy, and that is to make more just, more charitable, and, in a word, more virtuous those who in future are destined to guide and control them.   To this end every lover of his country and his race should arouse himself to a realizing sense of the great and overshadowing importance of properly educating and training up in the paths of virtue those who will soon have it in their power to either lift the nations into a loftier and purer atmosphere of truth, justice, religion, humanity, and fraternal love, or to plunge them into still deeper, darker, and fouler depths of crime, misery, and hopeless ruin.   The very first lesson we should teach our children is, that *man does not belong to himself* but to his Creator ; that he is as much the absolute property of his Maker as is the planet upon which he lives ; that in the vast economy of God's eternity each individual man is of far more value than the mightiest orb that rolls in space ; that his superior value over that of the material universe is not found in the superior quality of the clay of which his body is formed, but in his noble attributes of soul, which distinguish him as an immortal child of God and an heir to everlasting happiness.   He should be taught that worldly wealth, like worldly wisdom, is only truly valuable in proportion as it aids us in our journey from this land of misery, sin, sorrow, and death to our true country, and that it can only so aid us when used in the manner which its Great Author had in view in creating it ; and that unless properly used it becomes not a help but a positive hindrance to man's happiness both here and hereafter. But how is it possible for our children to learn in what manner their Maker would have them use property unless they first learn what is that Maker's will as regards themselves, and the duties which they owe both to Him and to their fellow-man? In other words, unless they learn, both in theory and in practice, so far as the same may be applicable to themselves, the great law of morality and religion which God has given to man for his government.

Without *this* knowledge, which is absolutely essential to enable them to make a proper use both of their worldly wisdom and worldly wealth, neither the one nor the other can be anything else than a source of danger and disaster both to themselves and to society.

He who, in the midst of his family, would place in the hands of his little child a Colt's revolver, both loaded and cocked, without first teaching him how to use and how not to use it, could only be regarded as either crazy or criminally foolish ; for he would be imperilling not only the life of his child, but that of every one within the reach of his pistol. Like unto him is the father who would store the mind of his child with worldly knowledge, or lavish upon him heaps of worldly wealth, without teaching him the law which God has given him for his guidance in the use of that knowledge or that wealth. And yet is not this precisely what the great body of American people, of all parties, creeds, and conditions, are doing to-day, both as regards their worldly knowledge and their worldly wealth? Is it not a fact that the great body of American people, while engaged, as it were, in a death struggle to grow rich and to leave their children rich, and while expending about $100,000,000.00 annually in order to cram the minds of these children with worldly knowledge, are at the same time not only taking no pains to instruct these little ones, or to cause them to be instructed, in the use which they ought and are in conscience bound to make both of their learning and their wealth, but are absolutely closing every avenue through which it is possible for them to receive such instruction? To fathers and mothers has the Almighty entrusted the sacred duty of teaching their little ones, or causing them to be taught, the great moral and religious truths which should always constitute their rule of action in their dealings both with God and their fellow-men. Then how lamentable is the fact that, instead of discharging this most sacred duty, vast multitudes of parents, of all creeds and classes, seem virtually to have conspired against God, against their children, and against society by denying to those children, through the medium of an anti-parental and Godless education, that very knowledge without which they can neither be true to themselves, **to their country, nor their God?**

We sincerely believe that moral and religious training are necessary for a child in order that it may know the proper use to make of this world's goods and this world's wisdom, but we hold that, amidst conflicting creeds and opinions on religious questions, it is not for the public but for the parental conscience to direct and control, by the aid of the best lights before it, the religious education of the child.   And it is not for the public but the parental purse to pay for that education.   We hold it to be a violation of religious liberty to force a man to pay for teaching a religion against which his conscience revolts, as well as it is to force him to accept such teachings for his children.   But under our existing educational system moral and religious teachings are as utterly impossible, without doing violence to somebody's conscience, as they would be in a law-established church.   Hence, the language of the 7th proposition of our platform (see *ante*) is so framed as to recognize the propriety and the liberty of imparting to children moral and religious education without cost to the public, and upon a basis objectionable to the conscience of none.

While we adhere to the proposition that religious education is essential both for the welfare of the child and the good of the State, yet we would not have the public to force such education on *any* child against the conscientious objection of its parents, because it is not the public but the parent that is the God-appointed guardian of the child; and hence, it is not the public, but the parental, conscience that must answer for any neglect to discharge the duties of so sacred a trust.   Direful as may be the result of allowing multitudes of children to grow up in the community with no knowledge of God or His holy law, yet it would be infinitely worse to allow the political State to domineer over the consciences of its citizens.   Moreover, it is undoubtedly true that, while oppressive laws sometimes make hypocrites, they never make men truly religious.   While we would allow even the infidel to educate his own children in his own way, for a still stronger reason we would desire that religionists of all creeds should enjoy a like privilege, for we regard almost any sort of religion which is sincerely professed, however erroneous in itself, as furnishing some sort of safeguard to society such as cannot be found in the utter scepticism of the atheist. Moroever, the faint and almost imperceptible glimmerings of religious truth which penetrate the dark caverns of the most erroneous of creeds, if faithfully followed, may serve to lead the honest searchers for light into the full blaze of open day.   Hence we can see no reason for any division or even for the least discord amongst

the friends of educational liberty and reform.   Even the confirmed
atheist, in standing upon our platform, will find himself at liberty,
without molestation from man, to indulge his dark dreams of anni-
hilation and despair, and to pour into the startled ear of his *own* child
the gloomy forebodings which blacken and make desolate the dreary
landscape of his own deluded soul.   But he must leave to his
neighbors at least the poor privilege of believing what *he* proclaims
himself unable to believe, and of pointing out to *their* little ones
the path of duty as the path which leads to a better land, where,
free from death, and sin, and sorrow, they may bask in the bright
sunshine of an eternal day.

We sincerely believe, in the very depths of our soul, that the only
lasting and effective cure for the crying wrongs with which greedy
monopolists, heartless tyrants, and unprincipled politicians are
scourging our country, and the only preventive against the still
more direful disaster with which we are threatened at the hands of
communistic demagogues, is to be found in a more widely spread
and deeper moral and religious sentiment among the people.   And
it is our earnest conviction that, in order to implant this sentiment
in the minds and hearts of our people, we require more of our
Saviour's gospel and less of Mr. Henry George's.

The Right Wing Individualist Tradition In America

An Arno Press/New York Times Collection

Bailie, William. **Josiah Warren:** The First American Anarchist. 1906.

Barber, Thomas H. **Where We Are At.** 1950.

Barnes, Harry Elmer. **Pearl Harbor After a Quarter of a Century.** Left and Right: A Journal of Libertarian Thought, Vol. IV. 1968.

Barnes, Harry Elmer. **In Quest of Truth and Justice:** De-Bunking the War Guilt Myth. 1928.

Barnes, Harry Elmer. **Selected Revisionist Pamphlets,** n.d. 1972.

Bromfield, Louis. **A New Pattern for a Tired World.** 1954.

Burgess, John W. **Recent Changes in American Constitutional Theory.** 1923.

Carroll, Charles Holt. **Organization of Debt into Currency:** and Other Papers. 1964.

Fleming, Harold M. **Ten Thousand Commandments:** A Story of the Antitrust Laws. 1951.

Flynn, John T. **As We Go Marching.** 1944.

Harris, George. **Inequality and Progress.** 1897.

Individualist Anarchist Pamphlets, 1867-1904. 1972.

Knight, Bruce Winton. **How to Run a War.** 1936. New Preface by Bruce Winton Knight.

Lane, Rose Wilder. **The Discovery of Freedom:** Man's Struggle Against Authority. 1943. New Foreword by Robert LeFevre. New Introduction by Roger Lea MacBride.

Left and Right: Selected Essays, 1954-1965. 1972.

The Libertarian Forum. 1969-1971. Murray N. Rothbard and Karl Hess, editors.

McGurrin, James. **Bourke Cockran:** A Free Lance in American Politics. 1948.

[La Monte, Robert Rives and H. L. Mencken.] **Men Versus The Man:** A Correspondence between Robert Rives La Monte, Socialist and H. L. Mencken, Individualist. 1910.

Montgomery, Zach[ariah], compiler. **The School Question:** From a Parental and Non-Sectarian Stand-Point. 1889.

Nock, Albert Jay. **Our Enemy, The State.** 1935.

Olds, Marshall. **Analysis of the Interchurch World Movement Report on the Steel Strike.** 1922.

Oppenheimer, Franz. **The State:** Its History and Development Viewed Sociologically. 1926.

Paterson, Isabel. **The God of the Machine.** 1943.

Phillips, C. A., T. F. McManus and R. W. Nelson. **Banking and the Business Cycle:** A Study of the Great Depression in the United States. 1937.

Schoeck, Helmut and James W. Wiggins, editors. **Scientism and Values.** 1960.

Scoville, John W. **Labor Monopolies or Freedom.** 1946.

Scoville, John and Noel Sargent, compilers. **Fact and Fancy in the T.N.E.C. Monographs.** 1942.

Snyder, Carl. **Capitalism The Creator:** The Economic Foundations of Modern Industrial Society. 1940.

Society Without Government: 1969-1970. 1972.
Tannehill, Morris and Linda and Jarret B. Wollstein.

Spooner, Lysander. **Let's Abolish Government,** 1852-1886. 1972.

Sprading, Charles T., editor. **Liberty and the Great Libertarians.** 1913.

Sumner, William Graham. **What Social Classes Owe to Each Other.** 1883.

Tolles, Frederick B. **George Logan of Philadelphia.** 1953.

Tucker, Benj[amin] R. **Instead of a Book:** By a Man Too Busy to Write One. 1893.

Vreeland, Hamilton, Jr. **Twilight of Individual Liberty.** 1944.

What Is Money? 1884-1963. 1972. Rothbard, Murray N. and I[saiah] W. Sylvester.

Williamson, Harold Francis. **Edward Atkinson:** The Biography of an American Liberal, 1827-1905. 1934.

Winston, Ambrose Paré. **Judicial Economics:** The Doctrine of Monopoly as Set Forth by Judges of the U.S. Federal Courts in Suits under the Anti-Trust Laws. 1957.

Date Due